the darwin Awards

ALSO BY WENDY NORTHCUTT

The Darwin Awards: Evolution in Action
The Darwin Awards II: Unnatural Selection

the darwin Awards

3

SURVIVAL OF THE FITTEST

Wendy Northcutt

DUTTON

DUTTON
Published by Penguin Group (USA) Inc.
375 Hudson Street, New York, New York 10014, U.S.A.
Penguin Books Ltd, Registered Offices: 80 Strand,
London WC2R 0RL, England
Penguin Books Australia Ltd, 250 Camberwell Road,
Camberwell, Victoria 3124, Australia
Penguin Books Canada Ltd, 10 Alcorn Avenue,
Toronto, Ontario, Canada M4V 3B2
Penguin Books (NZ) Ltd, Cnr Rosedale and Airborne Roads,
Albany, Auckland 1310, New Zealand

Published by Dutton, a member of Penguin Group (USA) Inc.

First Printing, October 2003
1 3 5 7 9 10 8 6 4 2

Illustrations by Malcolm McGookin and Jay "Zeebarf" Ziebarth.

 REGISTERED TRADEMARK—MARCA REGISTRADA

Library of Congress Cataloging-in-Publication Data has been applied for.

ISBN 0-525-94773-6

Printed in the United States of America
Set in Century Old Style and Weiss
Designed by Leonard Telesca

To Jacob, my favorite critic.

Contents

Introduction

Darwin Awards are not for everyone—only a select few earn this dubious distinction. Review the rules, the categories, and the evolutionary concepts underpinning the Darwin Awards.

CHAPTER 1
Law Enforcement: Crime Does Pay

In this chapter lawbreakers and law enforcers bump elbows in an informal competition to see who is best suited to lose the fight between good and evil. Inept bunglers from both sides of the law, from con artists to beat cops, from judges to crooks, astonish us with their casual disregard for the "natural laws" of physics.

CHAPTER 2
Men: Omega Male

In this chapter men meet their inner idiots as they test their testosterone levels by petting sharks, kissing snakes, and chasing beer cans. Only when it's too late do these would-be alpha males unexpectedly realize they're actually . . . omega males.

CHAPTER 3
Explosions: Short Sharp Shock

The destructive nature of fire and explosives has long been a lure for the more adventurous among us. But a fascination with all things flammable can lead to trouble, as shown by these eyebrow-searing tales of grenades, gelignite, bombs, gasoline, and flaming alcoholic desserts.

CHAPTER 4
Women: Female Finale

Our mothers warned us, "Don't run with scissors!" But they never warned us about shaving before a wet T-shirt contest, petting hippopotami and lion cubs, and other activities temporarily enjoyed by the following damsels in distress.

CHAPTER 5
Technology: Deus ex Machina

Deus ex machina (Latin for "God from the machine") is a theatrical term referring to a contrivance of playwrights faced by an irreconcilable plot line, who opt to have a god swoop down and untangle the situation. The heroes in this chapter contrive to find themselves in perilous juxtaposition to their machinery, situations from which they require divine intervention to survive—or not!

CHAPTER 6
Disqualified: Glory Days Gone

Not all submissions become Darwin Awards, and those that do
are sometimes disqualified when new information comes to
light, or extenuating circumstances are pointed out by readers. This chapter shows some of the stories that were nominated
but ultimately disqualified for violating one or more "Darwinian" rules.

Appendices

the
darwin Awards

You are a fluke of the universe
you have no right to be here,
and whether you can hear it or not,
the universe is laughing behind your back.

—"Deteriorata" by *National Lampoon*

Introduction

Darwin Awards are not for everyone—only a select few earn this dubious distinction. Review the rules, the categories, and the evolutionary concepts underpinning the Darwin Awards.

BEWARE
FALLING
NUMERALS

The Darwin Awards: Defined

Darwin Awards are bestowed upon individuals who improve our gene pool by removing themselves from it in a spectacularly stupid manner. They involve themselves in situations that a person with even a modicum of common sense would avoid, and their subsequent and predictable demise removes a set of judgment-impaired genes from circulation, thereby ensuring the long-term survival of the human race—which now contains one less idiot.

Every time a Darwin Award winner eradicates himself (or, occasionally, herself) from the population, we can breathe a sigh of relief, knowing that our descendants won't have to deal with—or breed with—the descendants of this mental midget, who lacks the ability to survive his own appallingly ill-conceived ideas.

Of necessity this honor is awarded posthumously, except in rare instances where a nominee eliminates only his ability to reproduce.

These stories are not mere tragic accidents. They are astonishing misapplications of judgment of such magnitude that the observer can only shake his head ruefully at the poetic justice dished out by fate to a deserving recipient.

The Darwin Awards commemorate the not-so-unexpected demise of a wood thief crushed by the overhead tree branch he methodically sawed in half while standing beneath it (page 37); two men competing to see who's the bravest of them all by holding lit fireworks in their mouths (page 55); a judge who pulled the pin of a live grenade introduced into evidence (page 41); and all the absentminded catastrophes caused by those who repeatedly stump us with their cluelessness.

Want to feel like a genius? The next time you feel foolish, stupid, or incompetent, seek out the *Darwin Awards* and read a few of these true tales of misadventure. You'll soon realize how brilliant you really are, compared with the morons featured on these pages.

And you will probably find yourself taking a few personal pledges while reading this book, such as: "I will keep pointy metal objects away from electrical wires." "I will not suck gasoline into a vacuum cleaner." "I will hold no fireworks in my mouth." "No sleeping in the road for me!"

There is an especial danger in new technology, which presents challenges that some people find insurmountable. The cover illustration shows the quintessential modern Darwin Award winner, holding a cell phone, intent on the wrong signals, and clueless in the face of impending doom. The image of a squashed cell-phone user typifies the absentminded human animal, unaware of dicey circumstances and headed for trouble.

Cell phones have become ubiquitous, but humans are still singularly ill equipped to use these devices safely. Although we have been communicating for millennia, we have not yet evolved the multitasking aptitude needed to talk on a cell phone while driving. Put one of these lethal instruments to the ear of the average driver, and a traffic accident is quite likely to

occur. In fact, accidents involving cell phones are too common to be eligible for a Darwin Award unless additional stupidity is present. "What's That Sound?" on page 160 and "(un) Armed and Dangerous" on page 190 are two sterling examples.

As more and more people remove themselves from the gene pool while using cell phones, the species as a whole will become better equipped to safely coexist with this new technology. As the population of cell-phone idiots is slowly depleted, one can imagine a golden day, far in the future, when cell phones are considered as safe to use as a faucet.

A 2002 Harvard study estimated that 6 percent of U.S. traffic accidents are caused by drivers talking on cell phones, resulting in 2,600 deaths and 330,000 injuries. In January 2003, the California Highway Patrol reported that cell phones are the leading cause of crashes attributed to driver distraction, a category that covers 10 percent of all crashes.

Reference: *San Jose Mercury News*

THE RULES

Now that the concept of the Darwin Awards has been explained, a discussion of the rules will not only elucidate their genesis, but also illuminate some of the more obscure questions that arise when evaluating nominees.

There are five basic rules:

Reproduction	Out of the gene pool!
Excellence	The event transcends common stupidity.
Self-selection	They did it to themselves!
Maturity	But not a child or handicapped person.
Veracity	Confirmed or, at least, plausible.

Reproduction

The candidate is no longer able to contribute to the gene pool.

The traditional method of satisfying this requirement is to cause one's own death. However, the occasional rebel opts for sterilization, which allows him more time to enjoy the dubious notoriety of winning this award.

The existence of offspring, though potentially deleterious to the gene pool, does not disqualify a nominee. Children inherit only half of each parent's genetic material and thus have their own chance to survive or snuff themselves—if, for instance, the "play with combustibles" gene has been passed along. If they *have* inherited the "play with combustibles" gene, but have *also* inherited a "use caution when . . . " gene, then they are potential innovators and possible assets to the human race. Therefore, each nominee is judged based on whether or not she has removed her own genes, without consideration to number of offspring or, in the case of an elderly winner, the likelihood of producing offspring regardless of an untimely demise.

Excellence

The candidate suffered an astounding lapse of judgment.

It takes a phenomenal failure of common sense to earn a Darwin Award. Common idiocies such as playing Russian roulette, falling off a boat, or sleeping next to a smoldering cigarette are not sufficient to win the dubious distinction of a Darwin. On the other hand, playing Russian roulette with land mines, jumping off a boat into shark-infested waters knowing you cannot swim, or sleeping with a smoldering cigarette under an oxygen tent . . . just might win you a Darwin Award!

It has been argued that more emphasis should be placed on the stupidity aspect, and less on the extreme nature of the stupidity. After all, humans are supposedly able to learn from their mistakes, and yet time and time again we manage to fall down stairs and drop radios into bathtubs. There is merit to this criticism, as natural selection is undoubtedly eliminating "bad driver" genes more rapidly than it's eliminating "grenade juggling" genes. However, it is not amusing to read dozens of stories about poor driving! Therefore, the Darwin Awards are given only to those who show their flagrant disregard for the laws of nature in a novel way.

Those who participate in extreme sports are not automatically eligible, as they knowingly assume an increased risk of death. They are, in a sense, correctly applying their judgment that the entertainment is worth the risk. However bizarre the sport, an additional misapplication of judgment must be present in order for the deceased to qualify for a Darwin Award.

Not a Darwin, but not safe either:

- Falling off a precipice while posing or pissing
- Warming aerosol cans or gasoline in the oven
- Whizzing on an electric rail or fence
- Being hit by a train or an automobile
- Smoking inside an oxygen tent
- Carbon monoxide poisoning
- Most autoerotic deaths

These circumstances are all too common!

Self-Selection

The candidate must be the cause of his own demise.

The humor of the Darwin Awards depends on the fact that the only victim is the nincompoop who planned the ill-fated scheme that resulted in his death. For that reason, the death of an innocent bystander rules out a nomination. *Self-removal* of incompetent genetic material is essential. One person cannot "give" another person a Darwin; rather, each person must earn the award based on his own ingenuity.

Oddly enough, those who commit suicide are not eligible for a Darwin Award, even though such a decision may be ill advised. A suicidal person is applying his judgment that life is not worth living, and the outcome is therefore expected. The spirit of the Darwin Awards, on the contrary, requires an element of surprise, when one departs from the gene pool by accident.

The death of an innocent bystander is not allowed, as it is not amusing. Suicides, whether or not they succeed, are not eligible. And anyone who dies while intentionally engaged in notoriety-seeking behavior is disqualified, as the Darwin Awards are not meant to encourage risk taking.

Maturity

The candidate must be able, and capable of sound judgment.

Some people, like children (whose judgment has not fully developed) or those who are born with physical or mental handicaps, are more susceptible to injury doing activities that an average adult can perform safely. Because the increased risk comes from an innate impediment, deaths that result are not amusing and not eligible for an award.

Also, children (typically below the age of sixteen) do not qualify, as it is commonly understood that they do not possess sufficient maturity and experience to make life-or-death judgments. The responsibility for their safety still resides with their parents and guardians.

The maturity rule is occasionally bent for a sufficiently humorous story. For instance, if a person confined to a wheelchair routinely travels by holding on to the fender of a speeding car, she is eligible for a Darwin Award when her wheelchair overturns on a freeway. Or if a woman chooses to impair her own judgment—for instance, by smoking marijuana before napping on a steep roof—she is eligible for a Darwin Award when she turns over in her sleep and rolls off the roof.

Veracity

The event must be verified.

The world is full of tales of wondrous stupidity, but in order to make the cut as a Darwin contender the tale must be true, not tall. Articles published by reputable news outlets, confirmed television and radio reports, and responsible eyewitnesses are considered valid sources. A chain email, an Internet humor 'zine, or an edited photograph, is not considered a valid source.

Depending on the plausibility of the story, more or less confirmation may be deemed sufficient to consider it verified. As the author has a finite amount of time to spend investigating the stories, a designation of "Confirmed by Darwin" means it has been verified to the best of her knowledge and is presumed—but not guaranteed—to be accurate.

THE CATEGORIES

There are three categories of stories in this book: Darwin Awards, Honorable Mentions, and Personal Accounts. All stories must be excellent examples of self-inflicted stupidity; the other three rules are flexible. Honorable Mentions and Personal Accounts usually don't meet the loss-of-reproduction rule. The veracity rule doesn't apply for Personal Accounts, which are by their nature unverified. And if a person is mature enough to submit her story as a Personal Account, age or other mental or physical impediments are of no concern.

Darwin Awards

> *Those whom life does not cure, death will.*
> —Cormac McCarthy

Darwin Awards are true examples of astounding stupidity leading to a loss of reproductive capacity, generally because the perpetrators are no longer alive. We do not take into account the unsettling possibility of the existence of cryogenically stored spermatozoa when selecting a Darwin Award recipient.

Honorable Mentions

> *He who hesitates . . . is sometimes saved.*
> —James Thurber

Honorable Mentions are foolish misadventures that, against all odds, stop short of the ultimate sacrifice. They illustrate the innovative spirit shown by a true Darwin Award candidate, without the unpleasant side effect of being deceased or, arguably worse, no longer able to reproduce.

Personal Accounts

> *Common sense is not so common.*
> —Voltaire

Personal Accounts were submitted by loyal readers blowing the whistle on stupidity—their own, or that of a spouse, neighbor, coworker, or (sometimes former) friend. The narratives are plausible but usually unverified. In some cases the people who submitted Personal Accounts have been identified with their permission, but this does not necessarily mean that they are directly associated with their Personal Accounts.

All Darwin Awards and Honorable Mentions are known or believed to be true. The phrase *Confirmed by Darwin* under the title generally indicates that a story was backed up by multiple submissions and by more than one reputable media source. *Unconfirmed by Darwin* indicates fewer credible submissions and the unavailability of direct confirmation of media sources. In unconfirmed Darwin Awards or Honorable Mentions, names have been changed and details of events have been altered to protect the innocent (and, for that matter, the guilty).

SURVIVAL OF THE FITTEST

Evolution is the process of species changing over time to better suit their environments. The mechanism of evolution was referred to as "survival of the fittest" by Alfred Russell Wallace, who is considered the codiscoverer of evolution. He used this phrase because he felt that the term coined by Charles Darwin, *natural selection,* incorrectly implied a directed force behind the selection.

In order for "survival of the fittest" to cause a species to evolve there are four requirements. The species must show variation, and that variation must be inheritable. Not all members of the population shall survive to reproduce, but the inherited characteristics of some members make them more likely to do so.

Inheritable Variation

Every species scientists have studied has been found to consist of individuals exhibiting a variety of traits. Numerous differences exist between even the most closely related individuals, from amoeba to zebra. Some variations are caused by environmental factors and are not inheritable; for instance, chronic food scarcity results in shorter humans. However, many variations are the result of different genetic instructions and are inherited. For example, even with ample food, short parents produce shorter children than tall parents. Only inheritable characteristics are subject to evolutionary pressures.

These inheritable characteristics are encoded in long strands of DNA. Populations constantly acquire new variations because the process by which DNA is copied is prone to infrequent but inevitable errors. The error rate of DNA transcription is not accidental, but rather is a carefully tuned variable that introduces an optimized amount of random mutation into a population. Because the vast majority of random mutations are deleterious, if they occur too frequently, the species would be too sickly to survive. If mutations occur too infrequently, the evolution rate would be too slow to keep up with the changing environment of a cooling Earth, or, later, with the competetion of other species adapting faster to their surroundings.

Some Succeed While Others Fail

Wild adult squirrels have two litters of three pups every summer, and they live about four years. Given these numbers, a single pair of squirrels could multiply to 63,967 trillion in thirty-three years if they all survived. (See figure on page 14.) That's more than enough squirrels to cover the entire surface of the planet! Obviously, most squirrels die before they produce nine children.

Because not all squirrels survive to reproduce, and because inherited traits play a role in which ones survive, there is a selective pressure that favors certain traits. If you spend time watching squirrels, you will see that some are fatter than others, some hide better, and some are more aggressive about obtaining food. The parents of each new generation are the most successful squirrels from the past summer. Thus, successful traits become more prevalent over time, and less successful traits eventually disappear.

Survival of the Fittest . . . Human?

That humans have evolved is evident from the fossil record, and that we have inherited successful traits is proved by the large worldwide population of humans. We meet all the requirements necessary to be involved in the race for "survival of the fittest." We show a wide variation of inheritable characteristics, and as the stories in this book attest, some members of the species are demonstrably less able to survive than others!

The Darwin Awards that follow show that Nature is still improving on the human design. But they also illustrate the creativity that distinguishes us from less adaptable species. The same innovative spirit that causes the downfall of the Darwin Award winners is also responsible for the social and scientific advances that make the human race great.

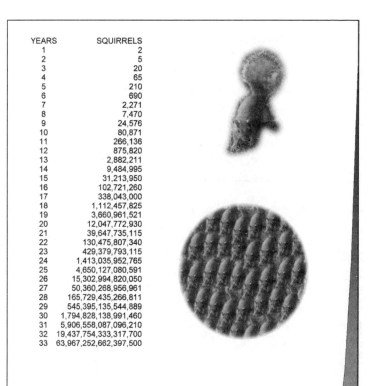

YEARS	SQUIRRELS
1	2
2	5
3	20
4	65
5	210
6	690
7	2,271
8	7,470
9	24,576
10	80,871
11	266,136
12	875,820
13	2,882,211
14	9,484,995
15	31,213,950
16	102,721,260
17	338,043,000
18	1,112,457,825
19	3,660,961,521
20	12,047,772,930
21	39,647,735,115
22	130,475,807,340
23	429,379,793,115
24	1,413,035,952,765
25	4,650,127,080,591
26	15,302,994,820,050
27	50,360,268,956,961
28	165,729,435,266,811
29	545,395,135,544,889
30	1,794,828,138,991,460
31	5,906,558,087,096,210
32	19,437,754,333,317,700
33	63,967,252,662,397,500

Surface area of Earth (EA) = 510,000,000,000,000 m2
Area covered by each squirrel (SA) = .1m x .2m = 0.02 m2
Number of squirrels needed to blanket the Earth = EA/SA
= 25,500,000,000,000,000 squirrels

Note: Calculation assumes that squirrels float.

CHAPTER 1

Law Enforcement:
Crime Does Pay

O would some Power the gift to give us,
To see ourselves as others see us!
It would from many a blunder free us,
And foolish notion.

—Robert Burns

In this chapter lawbreakers and law enforcers bump elbows in an informal competition to see who is best suited to lose the fight between good and evil. Inept bunglers from both sides of the law, from con artists to beat cops, from judges to crooks, astonish us with their casual disregard for the "natural laws" of physics.

BEWARE
FALLING
NUMERALS

DISCUSSION: PICKING THE WINNERS

Contenders for the Darwin Award are selected based on the five criteria of death, self-selection, excellence, maturity, and veracity. But there's more to the selection process than one person writing stories and making a dry comparison with the rules. The selection is a participatory event, a community celebration of the humor found in the inevitable results of foolish choices! Here's how the entire process works.

Submission

A Darwin Award begins its life as a submission to the website. The nominations come from around the world, and without these submissions there would be no Darwin Awards. Enthusiasts are encouraged to keep a sharp lookout for potential contenders in their neighborhoods and local newspapers. If the event is written into a story that highlights its humorous aspects, rather than simply a bare link or newspaper quote, so much the better! Amusingly presented stories are more likely to pass the triple hurdles of moderation, public vote, and Wendy's review.

The current system was initiated in January 2002, as I could no longer keep up with the thousands of emails sent every month. The correspondence included submissions, additional information, debates on the merits of candidates, flames, commendations, requests for vaguely remembered stories, and so forth. Much as I enjoy reading these emails, the quantity was simply too much for one person to deal with. In fact, I still have thousands of unread emails and submissions! That's why the more formal submission system described herein was devised. Now submissions receive quicker treatment, and fewer good stories languish in the dusty recesses of an overflowing inbox.

Moderator Review

Each submission is reviewed by a team of volunteer moderators who decide whether it's a potential Darwin Award, Honorable Mention, or Personal Account. Anywhere from two to five moderators rate each story before it's moved from the moderation queue to the public Slush Pile. Submissions that don't make the cut are usually repeats, bizarre or macabre stories, or illustrations of poetic justice, rather than examples of Darwinian self-selection. These stories are placed in the public Slush Pile Rejects area.

As the graph illustrates, an average of five hundred stories are submitted per month, and approximately one in six is accepted into the Slush Pile. When a particularly sensational story appears in the news, it can be submitted hundreds of times. The spike in January 2003 was due to the shooting death of a man who decided to beat his misbehaving dog with a loaded gun. The spike in July 2002 was caused by two men fighting over who would go to heaven and who to hell; a shotgun was used to solve the argument. The September 2002 spike resulted in the Darwin Awards "Slip Sliding Away," on page 53, and "A Rocky Roll" on page 30.

Monthly Darwin Award Submissions

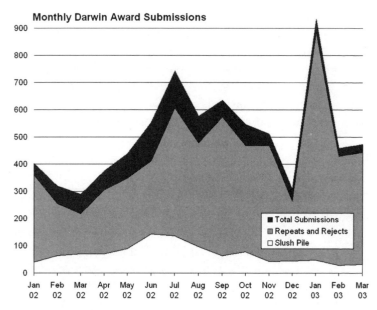

Public Review

The stories, with moderator scores and comments appended, are transferred to the website for public review. They land in the Slush Pile or the Slush Pile Reject area, and the submitter is notified by email. The decision may be appealed; however, the moderators are fairly experienced, so stories are only infrequently salvaged from the Reject area. It is rarer yet for a story to be removed from the Slush Pile, as only one in three will, in any case, be moved to the permanent archive. A submission will occasionally be removed for privacy reasons, or if it is the cause of many complaints.

Readers read and rate the stories in the Slush Pile on a scale from 0 to 10, with each story receiving approximately eighty votes, although the number ranges from fifteen to five hundred, depending on how much interest it evokes.

Vote on Slush Pile Submissions!
www.DarwinAwards.com/slush

Wendy's Review

After at least a month of public review, I sort the Slush Pile based on popularity and begin reading through the submissions for that month. I refer to the moderator comments and decide whether each story is novel enough, and amusing enough, to write into a Darwin Award, Honorable Mention, or Personal Account. Approximately ten to fifteen stories per month are selected to enter the permanent archive.

The Final Cut

But that's not the end of the process! In fact, it's a new beginning, for stories in the archive enjoy a far greater audience than when they first appeared in the Slush Pile. Visitors cast five million votes per month, and mistakes, corrections, and confirmations are frequently reported. Stories that are particularly comment-worthy are linked to a discussion thread in the Philosophy Forum. The Darwin Awards are continually updated (or removed) based on new information, and this final

review process continues for as long as the story remains on the website.

The accounts in this book have all been subject to this public scrutiny and are accurate to the best of my knowledge. But because the Darwin Awards are dynamically modified, they are not guaranteed to be entirely accurate, nor in their final form.

The last chapter in this book features stories that have been disqualified, and the reasons for the disqualifications. Most appeared in the website archive, but were later removed based on this final public review.

As you read the tales contained herein, keep in mind the lengthy submission process, and the care with which each gem was culled from dozens of competitors and honed to its current form.

DARWIN AWARD: CONVINCE THE JURY

Confirmed by Darwin

16 JUNE 1871

Proof that the only good lawyer is a dead lawyer.

Clement Vallandigham was a well-known Northern Democrat who campaigned for states' rights during the Civil War. In 1863 Vallandigham was convicted of treason for his speeches attacking the administration of President Lincoln. He was banished to the South, where he continued to voice his political views.

After the war Vallandigham became a lawyer. In his last appearance in the courtroom he represented a client on trial for murder. The accused man's defense was that the victim had drawn his own gun in a fashion that caused it to fire, killing himself. To prove the defense argument, Vallandigham demonstrated the victim's method of drawing a gun—using the loaded evidence gun as his prop. The firearm went off, and he lost his life—but proved his case!

Reference: Klement, Frank L. *The Limits of Dissent: Clement Vallandigham and the Civil War.* Fordham, Mass.: Fordham University Press, 1998.

Reader Comments:
"A mind is a terrible thing to waste."
"If only all criminals were so accommodating."
"He couldn't extrapolate from the lesson,
Don't run with scissors."
"This will keep the prison population down."
"An argument against gun control."

DARWIN AWARD: FAULTY AIM FATAL

Confirmed by Darwin

7 MARCH 2002, COLORADO

When Gerald was pulled over by police for erratic driving, he decided it was better to flee from the stolen car on foot, rather than face possible jail time for a parole violation. This was the first of two successive mental lapses. Gerald's actual thoughts are unknown, but *may* have been something like this: *The officers are merely suspicious and alert now . . . why not make them hot, sweaty, tired, and angry, by leading them on a wild chase through dark alleys and fields?*

During the subsequent foot chase Gerald attempted to dissuade officers from the pursuit by firing a 9mm Ruger semiautomatic handgun blindly over his shoulder. This was the second illustration of a potential mental deficiency: *Officers are running behind me. They have guns. I have a gun! They have eyes in the front of their heads, so they can see to aim at me. I don't have eyes in the back of my head, so I'll fire wildly behind me and see what happens!*

Unfortunately, Gerald appears to have been one of those folks who can't chew gum and walk at the same time. Or at least he couldn't flee and fire at the same time. While discharging the weapon over his shoulder, Gerald managed to shoot himself in the head, bringing the chase to a sudden conclusion.

Four shots were fired, none by the officers, who found Gerald's pistol next to his fallen body. Gerald was transported to a local hospital where he expired the following day, thus removing a set of genes deficient in both judgment and coordination from the gene pool.

Reference: *Colorado Springs Gazette-Telegraph,* 9news.com

DARWIN AWARD: CHAIN SAW INSURANCE
Confirmed by Darwin
JANUARY 2002, ITALY

Some people will do anything for money.

Andreas, a twenty-three-year-old bouncer from Italy, was found lying in a pool of blood near a country road. Police initially mistook him for a victim of sadistic mutilation. His left leg had been nearly severed by a chain saw. His last act was an emergency call to operators, who heard only a "death rattle." By the time help arrived, copious bleeding had drained his body of blood.

A violent attack on an innocent man? Not quite.

Andreas was the victim of his own conspiracy to commit an insurance scam. In order to reap half a million dollars from numerous insurance policies, permanent disability was all that was required. So Andreas convinced his cousin to cut off his left leg with a chain saw. Andreas relied on his knowledge of first aid to survive the chainsaw incident.

His twenty-nine-year-old cousin confessed that he was the designated assailant, and that he had attacked—and inadvertently killed—the younger man in a mutually planned, high-stakes fraud that went badly awry.

The attack took place near a country lay-by. The cousin sawed Andreas's leg below the knee, severing a major artery. The gambit for permanent disability was successful, in a sense, yet it was timed too close for Andreas to survive. Emergency crews found him dead, and his cousin fled, tossing the chain saw in a river on the way out of town.

Andreas's death was a classic example of fate noticing those who buy chain saws.

Reference: www.cnnItalia.it, *Glas*, Yugoslav daily,
La Nazione, news.bcc.co.uk, Ananova

An insurance adjuster commented, "This reminds me of a claim where the chap purposely cut off his little finger. We refused it, because he had not lost the use of his limb below the wrist. He apparently didn't follow our reasoning, as six months later, he submitted another claim after axing off the next finger. We still refused the claim!"

DARWIN AWARD: TRUCK STOP
Confirmed by Darwin
31 MARCH 2002, BANGLADESH

Six highway robbers, who had apparently watched too many gangster movies, were caught in their own trap when they blocked a bypass with their car at midnight in a ploy to garner victims. The driver of an oncoming truck carrying a cargo of cows was unable to halt his heavy vehicle in time. The truck rolled right through the blockade, crushing the car and its scheming occupants. Five *dacoits* died, and the sixth was critically wounded. A cow was also killed in the accident.

Reference: *Dhaka (Bangladesh) Independent*

A *dacoit* is a member of a gang of robbers in India. *Dacoity* is the practice of (armed) gang robbery.

DARWIN AWARD: ANTLERS AHOY!

Confirmed by Darwin

1985, MONTANA

Two locals decided to increase their income by illegally transporting shed elk antlers out of Yellowstone Park. The antlers sell for about seven dollars a pound, and a big set can weigh thirty pounds, making their theft a lucrative venture.

The two men, dollar signs in their eyes, thought long and hard about the best way to get the largest haul of antlers out of the park without being observed. Cars were too risky because there was a ranger checkpoint on the roads. Backpacks couldn't carry enough to make it worth their while. They decided to use a boat.

Well, not exactly a boat. A rubber raft.

These two entrepreneurs decided to take the raft on a nighttime voyage on the Gardiner River, which runs out of Yellowstone and through the town of Gardiner, to minimize the chance of being spotted.

After loading the raft to the bursting point with pointy antlers, the men pushed off and began their journey. It was late springtime, so the river, hazardous in all seasons, now had twice the normal flow of water. They hadn't gone far before they hit some treacherous rapids, and the bouncing antlers punctured the raft.

Deprived of transportation, the men had to fend for themselves against the current. One of the antler thieves swam to shore, hiked the road, and hitched a ride into town. The other was not so lucky. A week later he floated onto a beach used by local sunbathers.

This story was confirmed in an unusual way.
The primary source of information is an eye-witness account by a person who gave the survivor a ride into town, and later found the body on the beach. But the story is also described in a book, *Death in Yellowstone,* by Lee H. Whittlesey, published in 1995. This book cites articles in the *Billings Gazette* ("Body of Antler Smuggler Recovered") and the *Livingston Enterprise* ("Gardiner Horn Hunter Presumed Drowned in Park"). I have chosen to use details provided by the eyewitness. While the fact of the antler theft is confirmed, there are some discrepancies regarding the exact nature of the undertaking. According to the book, a man loaded 250 pounds of antlers onto a large raft, then tied it to his own one-man raft, which later overturned on the river.

DARWIN AWARD: SKELETON KEY

Confirmed by Darwin

2001

Another would-be thief has been discovered languishing as a pile of bones, this one uncovered by an artisan brick mason. The protruding foot and leg bones found during building renovations belonged to a thief who had tried to rob a gift shop by way of the second-floor chimney fifteen years before, speculated bemused authorities. Maybe he should have tried a skeleton key.

Reference: *Natchez (Mississippi) Democrat, Chicago Tribune*

Caution: Natural Selection at Work

DARWIN AWARD: A ROCKY ROLL

Confirmed by Darwin

29 AUGUST 2002, WASHINGTON

An innovative petty crime spree turned into a Darwinian opportunity when a Vancouver man fell out of a minivan while throwing rocks. Five men had been denting mailboxes and terrorizing moving cars with their low-tech missiles, when twenty-three-year-old John decided he needed a wider range of targets. As the Ford Aerostar cruised through a residential neighborhood, he left his compatriots at the windows while he opened the sliding door. One mighty throw later, he pitched through the opening, struck his head on the pavement, and suffered the ultimate penalty for his crime: stone-cold death.

Reference: www.KGW.com, Northwestc NewsChannel 8

Astoundingly, the deceased may not be legally accountable for his own death. A spokesperson for the sheriff's office said that the driver, the person ultimately responsible for the vehicle, could be charged with a range of offenses, from allowing a passenger to ride without a seat belt to vehicular homicide.

DARWIN AWARD: BOOBY TRAPS TRAP BOOB

Confirmed by Darwin

NOVEMBER 2002, BELGIUM

A retired engineer living in Charleroi booby-trapped his home with the intention of killing his estranged family, but died himself after inadvertently triggering one of his own devices.

At first police assumed that the seventy-nine-year-old had committed suicide, as he was found alone with a bullet wound in his neck. Then a detective missed a bullet by inches when he opened a booby-trapped wooden chest. Police beat a hasty retreat from the property and called in military experts.

The experts deciphered an enigmatic series of scribbled clues to locate nineteen death traps in walls, ceilings, and household objects. A pile of booby-trapped dinner plates was revealed, for example, by the clue "Cheaper by the Dozen," a reference to a film in which a child throws a plate at someone's head. Police speculated that the notes were intended to assist his failing memory.

Other traps included numerous concealed shotguns triggered by threads, and an exploding crate of beer set to detonate once a certain number of bottles was removed. It took three weeks to crack nineteen of the twenty clues, and experts were forced to admit defeat on the final note: "The 12 Apostles are ready to work on the pebbles." Said one expert, "We have never come across anything like it before. It was all fiendishly clever."

True to form, the "fiendishly clever" but careless Darwin Award winner was described by neighbors as a taciturn but harmless man who enjoyed puttering in his garage. But relatives say he had never forgiven his wife for divorcing him twenty years earlier.

Police believe he began installing the traps four years before the incident, after losing a lengthy battle to keep his home.

Reference: *Daily Telegraph* (London), *The Age* (Melbourne, Australia), The Associated Press

Questions have been raised regarding the soundness of this nomination. Perhaps the man was obsessive to the point of insanity, or suffering from senile dementia, and therefore not capable of sound judgment. At age seventy-nine, and possessed of fourteen children and thirty-seven grandchildren, his continuing influence on the gene pool was assured. And furthermore, the workers who discovered and dismantled the devices were placed in harm's way, thus innocent bystanders *could* have been injured. However, the judges have decided that the notion of diminished mental capacity is merely speculative, that offspring and advanced age are not a bar to a nomination, that no innocent bystanders *were* injured, and that the magnitude of his actions make it imperative that he be given a Darwin Award.

DARWIN AWARD: CAVEAT EMPTOR

Confirmed by Darwin
4 FEBRUARY 2002, NEW MEXICO

Let the buyer beware.

Police say three men tried to rob an Albuquerque man who had placed a newspaper ad to sell a gun. The robbers arranged a meeting, then beat and sprayed Mace on the gun seller in an attempt to steal the weapon.

Surprise! The gun seller was ipso facto a gun owner. Eighteen-year-old Carlos intercepted a bullet and died before rescue crews arrived.

One can understand the mistake of robbing a man who unexpectedly pulls out a gun and shoots—but if a robber singles out a victim because he is selling a gun, there's no excuse for being surprised to discover he is armed.

As a Darwinian bonus there's a fairly good chance that the eighteen-year-old has not yet reproduced. . . .

Reference: KOAT TV, TheNewMexicoChannel.com

DARWIN AWARD: JET SKI SPREE

Confirmed by Darwin

26 JULY 2001, NEVADA

Sometimes fate has perfect vision. Two men found dead at Lake Tahoe were presumed to be homicide victims—one disfigured by severe facial wounds and the other apparently shot—until investigators discovered that they were actually victims of their own larcenous tendencies. The men had stolen a jet ski from a marina, but, unfamiliar with the lay of the land and piloting in pitch darkness, they had crashed at high speed into a nearby dock. One man died instantly from a broken neck; the other crawled to shore where he, too, expired.

Reference: TheKCRAChannel.com and The Associated Press

Dumb, Dumber, Darwin

DARWIN AWARD: RISKY REENACTMENT
Unconfirmed by Darwin
23 OCTOBER 1993, ILLINOIS

A police officer trying to show another patrolman how their fellow officer accidentally killed himself, accidentally killed *himself* while reenacting the shooting incident a week later. The twenty-year veteran forgot to unload his .357 Magnum, shot himself in the stomach, and died in a car crash while driving himself to the hospital.

**Death comes to all men,
but some just can't wait.**

DARWIN AWARD: RETURN TO TREES FAILS
Confirmed by Darwin
18 FEBRUARY 2002, HAWAII

Millennia after an evolving human species descended from the trees, thirty-year-old Joshua reversed the process, removing himself from the gene pool while perched in a tree. Joshua had hiked several miles onto a ranch and climbed a koa tree under cover of darkness, intent upon stealing a branch of the expensive native hardwood. To his credit he was smarter than a classic cartoon character and didn't make the mistake of cutting the branch supporting him. However, he was not smart enough to avoid cutting a branch directly above his head. The severed limb struck and killed him. Authorities found his body still in the tree, suspended twenty feet off the ground.

Reference: *Honolulu Star-Bulletin*

Famous Last Words:
It seemed like a good idea at the time

DARWIN AWARD: FLAMINGO GUNFIGHT
Unconfirmed by Darwin
30 DECEMBER 2000, MISSOURI

A Kansas City police officer was in a bar called the Flamingo, looking forward to a musical performance by his friends. He had only just arrived when a man ran into the bar and announced that he'd been robbed in the parking lot, as had a second victim!

The officer elicited the details of the crime, called for backup, and ran outside, assuming the villain would be long gone. To his surprise the suspect was still sitting in the pickup truck he had recently carjacked. The officer approached the man with his gun and his shield drawn for identification.

It turned out that the suspect had stolen a vehicle with a manual transmission, but was unable to drive a stick shift. When he saw the officer, he tried to flee but had trouble putting the truck into reverse. Only the sound of grinding gears disturbed the quiet night, until the officer hauled the incompetent criminal from the immobile car.

At that point he challenged the officer to a gunfight—and was quickly dispatched by the startled officer. A check of the perpetrator's gun revealed it was almost fully loaded, except for the most important round—the one in the chamber.

There are two morals to this story: If you steal a car, learn how to drive a stick shift first; and if you challenge a police officer to a duel, be prepared to meet your maker.

Reference: *Kansas City Star*

DARWIN AWARD: TIRED AMMO

Unconfirmed by Darwin

1990S, SOUTHERN UNITED STATES

A small-time hoodlum, about to be even smaller, broke into the home of a World War II veteran and stole the old man's .45-caliber automatic pistol, a weapon used in battle in the 1940s. The hoodlum then reported directly to a local convenience store and brandished his new pistol.

The cashier, a sensible employee, followed orders and handed over the minimal contents of the cash register. The security video showed our thug taking the money and turning to leave, when he suddenly decided not to risk leaving a witnesses behind—other than the security camera, that is. He leveled the pistol at the cashier and pulled the trigger.

"Click!"

At this unexpected development the puzzled crook looked straight down the barrel of the antique weapon and uttered his last words. "What the . . . ?"

It turned out that the WWII veteran kept WWII-vintage ammunition in his WWII-vintage pistol. Priming caps lose their "spontaneous" nature as they age, particularly if stored improperly, causing what's referred to as a hangfire: The primer smolders into a delayed ignition.

Such was the case here.

Just as the puzzled crook turned the barrel to point squarely at his own eyeball, the hangfired primer detonated, sending a half-inch chunk of lead directly into his skull.

The body could only be identified by fingerprints.

The police officer who had responded to the original gun burglary call was also summoned to the scene of the armed robbery. He picked up the .45, verified the serial number, and returned it to the WWII veteran. Case closed!

All people improve the gene pool, some by birth, some by their demise.

HONORABLE MENTION: SHORT ARM OF THE LAW
Confirmed by Darwin
MAY 2002, PAKISTAN

Lack of judicial restraint leads to a judicial error.

Usually it's the criminal, not the judge, who attempts to take himself out of the gene pool. But not in this twist on a familiar tale! A man accused of possessing a hand grenade challenged police to produce it at his trial. When the police brought the grenade into the courtroom, the defendant claimed it was not real. The judge absentmindedly took the grenade in his hand while listening to arguments—and pulled the pin! He was injured but survived, no doubt with improved judgment.

Reference: Agence France-Presse, *Khaleej Times*

**The difference between genius and idiocy?
Genius has its limits.**

HONORABLE MENTION: FAMILIAR KNICKERS
Confirmed by Darwin
OCTOBER 2001, NORWAY

A drunken robber, masked in his own underpants, presented a bank teller with a demand note and absconded with the money. But his gains were short lived: His wife's name was written on the reverse side of the note paper.

When apprehended in his home the next day, the forty-seven-year-old man said he didn't remember committing the robbery, but had a suspicion he'd been up to no good when he saw a picture of the robber in the morning paper. The masked man was wearing a hauntingly familiar pair of underwear on his head, and our forgetful thief found an unexplained wad of cash in his pocket.

Reference: Reuters, *Bergensavisen, Ottawa Citizen*

Dysfunctional Genomics

HONORABLE MENTION: I SHOT THE SHERIFF

Confirmed by Darwin

19 MARCH 2002, OHIO

Sometimes it hurts to "cover your ass."

"Shots fired, shots fired—I'm hit," a police chief radioed to headquarters. The fifty-two-year-old officer reported that he'd been shot in the leg during an incident that began as a routine traffic stop.

He had pulled over a rusted Chevrolet missing its license plates, but before he could emerge from his police cruiser, the driver had opened fire and put a bullet through the windshield. The suspect then charged the chief, who was shot in the leg during the ensuing struggle.

A statewide manhunt was launched to locate the gunman, described as a white, bearded male, six feet four inches tall and weighing 195 pounds.

One week later the law-enforcement team nabbed their man: the police chief himself, who confessed to fabricating the entire event to hide the fact that he had accidentally fired his rifle through the windshield of his police car. To cover up his blunder he drove out to a county road, radioed in for help, and fired his weapon to make it sound like there was trouble at the scene of a traffic stop. Then he accidentally fired his weapon again, this time striking his own leg.

To inadvertently discharge a weapon once might be considered a simple accident, but doing so twice in one night earns this police chief an Honorable Mention. Had that shot ricocheted . . . he might have won a Darwin Award instead!

Reference: Cleveland-Akron Channel 5 News

**Against stupidity, the gods themselves
contend in vain.
—Friedrich von Schiller**

HONORABLE MENTION: PAROLE CALLING CARD

Unconfirmed by Darwin

9 AUGUST 2001, SOUTH AFRICA

A careless thief left behind the most incriminating of evidence—his parole card—in a pair of jeans he discarded after changing into stolen clothes. He made off with jewelry, cutlery, and electronics, but was quickly apprehended using the information provided by the parole card. Fingerprints found at the scene of the crime matched those on the card, and he was jailed for the botched home robbery.

Reference: South Africa Independent Online News

Tales From the Shallow End of the Gene Pool

HONORABLE MENTION: WEST VIRGINIA ALIBI
Confirmed by Darwin
12 JAN 2001, WEST VIRGINIA

A suspected bank robber's alibi for the crime placed him in hot water, when he claimed to have been buying heroin in another state at the time of the robbery. He gave Charleston police a hotel receipt by way of proof, and sure enough, they found eighty-four packets of heroin when they searched the room.

Reference: Associated Press

You can learn a lot from a dummy.

PERSONAL ACCOUNT: COPPER CLOD
15 AUGUST 2000, AUSTRALIA

I work for the Canberra Fire Brigade. One of the more interesting jobs I've attended was an explosion reported at 1:30 one morning. We found an abandoned pub that had collapsed into wreckage. Three days later, while removing debris, we located a Darwin Awards contender beneath the rubble and worked out what had happened.

The man was a licensed plumber who wanted to save money on supplies. He was inside the old pub, cutting sections of copper pipe, when he inadvertently sliced through the gas main and sparked a huge explosion that sent glass and roof tiles hurtling as far as five hundred meters away.

Shouldn't a plumber know the difference between a water pipe and a gas main? Saving a few bucks cost him his life!

Reference: Anonymous Personal Account; *Canberra Times*

CHAPTER 2

Men: Omega Male

*It may be that your sole purpose in life
is simply to serve as a warning to others.*

—Anonymous

In this chapter men meet their inner idiots as they test their testosterone levels by petting sharks, kissing snakes, and chasing beer cans. Only when it's too late do these would-be alpha males unexpectedly realize they're actually . . . omega males.

DISCUSSION: GLOWING GREEN MONKEYS

Researcher: "I'd like a grant."
Foundation: "No."
Researcher: "I'm the glowing green monkey guy."
Foundation: "Why didn't you say so? Here's your grant!"

In 2001 scientists inserted a jellyfish gene into a monkey, creating what the media referred to as "glowing green monkeys." The jellyfish gene produces Green Fluorescent Protein, or GFP, which fluoresces under ultraviolet light. GFP is a commonly used marker to test for cells that have successfully incorporated a more useful gene. Although the monkeys did not look unusual to the naked eye, their hair did glow green under UV light, showing that the DNA marker had indeed made the leap from an invertebrate into a mammal, and that it happened to have been inserted near the gene that codes for hair color.

The glowing green monkey made a splash in the national media, but in scientific circles it was considered rather pedestrian. It simply showed that the same techniques used for years on other mammals would also work on primates, a notion that had previously been assumed but not confirmed. While the green monkey was not useful in and of itself—the inserted gene is only a marker—there are many interesting uses for transgenic animals and gene transfer technology.

Transgenic animals have been available to scientists for many years. Simple one-celled animals such as bacteria and yeast have been producing foreign proteins for decades. Millions of transgenic mice, rabbits, and goats are used in laboratories each year, and even more are raised on farms.

Of what use are all these mutants?

Transgenic animals are used to model human diseases. Such research has resulted in a deeper understanding of spina bifida, multiple sclerosis, cancers, Alzheimer's disease, cystic fibrosis, rheumatoid arthritis, and other ills that plague mankind. Improved knowledge based on animal models has resulted in effective new therapies for many diseases.

Transgenic animals have been created to improve their agricultural utility. We now have sheep producing thicker wool coats, fish growing larger faster, and cows giving more milk, thanks to the introduction of foreign genes. Genes from Alaskan fish that can survive in cold waters have been transferred to other fish species to confer resistance to cold. Scientists have even developed transgenic cows that produce milk with less lactose or cholesterol!

Transgenic animals are used to create biological pharmaceuticals. Bacteria and yeast produce insulin, human and animal growth hormones, and other drugs. But many bioactive proteins cannot be expressed in one-celled organisms because they depend upon protein processing found in more complex animals. Transgenic sheep express a protein in their milk that that treats emphysema. Transgenic cows can be milked for Factor IX, a clotting factor for hemophiliacs. Transgenic goats produce tissue plasminogen activator, an anticlotting drug used on heart-attack victims.

If the uses described above aren't amazing enough, here's one that sounds like it's straight from the pages of a lurid science-fiction novel: Transgenic pigs are being developed to be blood and organ donors for humans. Pig organs have already been used as "bridge organs" for patients who need an immediate transplant when none is available, but because humans reject foreign proteins, the animal transplant must soon be replaced with a proper human organ. But researchers are substituting human proteins for the pig's natural proteins, in hopes of creating animal organs suitable for permanent transplant.

Primate research—the glowing green monkey—brings us a step closer to inserting foreign genes into humans. For some that thought evokes the specter of a race of superhumans grown from made-to-order babies. But scientists prefer to use transgenic research to better the human condition, rather than bring a comic book fantasy to life. It's far more likely that the first transgenic humans will be those permanently cured of genetic diseases such as Huntington's disease and sickle-cell anemia.

Take comfort in the knowledge that humans have been performing genetics experiments for centuries. How else could we have bred a Chihuahua from a wolf? If transgenic research gives us nothing else, perhaps it will give us humans who express the Green Fluorescent Protein and glow green under the black lights at dance clubs.

References:
www.frame.org.uk/Transgenics.htm
www.agwest.sk.ca/event_inf_may95.shtml
www.nexiabiotech.com/HTML/technology/bele.shtml
www.actionbioscience.org/biotech/margawati.html

DARWIN AWARD: SLIP SLIDING AWAY

Confirmed by Darwin
8 SEPTEMBER 2002, ITALY

"Hey, watch this!" A fifty-three-year-old Glasgow man on tour in the Alps, attempting what police described as a bizarre stunt, attached a climber's snap hook to an unused overhead tram cable and attempted to manually ride down the mountain. But the mountain was steep, gravity was constant, and he was unable to moderate his rate of descent. He accelerated out of control and within seconds crashed against the rocks, and proceeded to bash his way two hundred meters down the slope before impacting a pylon. Reports state that several people attempted to stop him from riding down the cable. He should have listened to their advice. When he came to rest, he was DOA.

Reference: BBC News, *The Scotsman*

**Famous Last Words:
Watch this!**

DARWIN AWARD: FOOLISH COURAGE

Unconfirmed by Darwin
1 JANUARY 2002, BRAZIL

The game of Russian roulette, long a breeding ground for natural selection, was improved upon by two men with a unique approach to self-destruction.

On New Year's Eve, Claudio and his friend were befogged by *pinga*, a traditional Brazilian liquor, when they began playing a Russian-roulette variant using holiday fireworks. Their version of the game consisted of placing fireworks in their mouths, then lighting the fuses and competing to see who would delay longest before spitting out the firework.

The man—dare we call him "winner?"—who discarded the explosive closest to the point of detonation was the victor of this battle of wills. Their blatant disregard for personal safety was matched only by their foolish bravery. Claudio was our winner, holding one of the fireworks in his mouth a bit too long and thereby earning praise for his "courage" at his funeral.

Reference: *O Estado de São Paulo*

> **Confirmed reports of men who survived "Fireworks Roulette" should warn participants that living with the disfiguring aftermath takes far more courage.**

DARWIN AWARD: MORTAL INSULT
Confirmed by Darwin
1992, CALIFORNIA

Rattler got your tongue?

Snakes flick their forked tongues in the air to "smell" the world, collecting molecules and analyzing them by pressing their tongue tips into small olfactory pits. An inebriated twenty-year-old man, apparently unaware of this biological fact, took umbrage when a wild rattlesnake stuck out its tongue at him. Tit for tat! He held the rattler in front of his face and stuck his tongue out right back at it. The snake expressed its displeasure at this turn of events by biting the conveniently offered body part. The toxic venom swelled the man's face and throat, choking him to death.

Reference: *San Francisco Chronicle*

Experts debate which species of venomous snake is most dangerous. It depends on how irritable the snake is, the toxicity of its venom, whether it delivers the venom reliably, and how likely the snake is to come into contact with humans.

Rattlesnakes certainly rank among the most dangerous of snakes. They often live in close proximity to humans, and some species can be quite irritable, particularly when they are cornered. Rattlesnakes have long, folding fangs that deliver venom deeply into the body. However, some rattlers fail to inject venom into the bite as frequently as twenty-five percent of the time. Young rattlesnakes are more likely to deliver a full load of venom and are therefore more dangerous than their elders.

For those who value their looks as much as their life: Remember, rattlesnake venom is disfiguring as well as deadly.

DARWIN AWARD: I CAN'T SWIM!

Unconfirmed by Darwin
1 JULY 2002, CANADA

Talk about being out of one's depth.

The population of Thunder Bay, a beautiful city located on the shores of Lake Superior, was decreased by one Darwin Award candidate over the long Canada Day weekend. The story takes place on Obonga Lake, a hundred miles north of Thunder Bay.

The holiday weekend was a scorcher, with temperatures in the high nineties. Our candidate went for a cooling boat ride with his wife and children, but the cool breeze did not suffice, so he turned off the motor and dived into the lake.

Plunging into Canada's northern lakes is risky. During the summer a thin surface layer of warmer water covers the colder depths. Diving into one of these thermoclines can result in paralysis when you hit the icy water a few feet below the surface. But that's not what happened to our diver.

His first error was more basic: He was unable to swim and wasn't wearing a life jacket, the logical attire of a boating nonswimmer.

His second error was neglecting to consider the effect of the wind, which was not only pushing the boat away from him but also foiling efforts to throw him a life preserver, which is buoyant in water, and necessarily lightweight.

And his third error was in not having taught his wife to pilot the boat, so she was unable to start the engine, drive over, and rescue him.

The people in the boat waved their arms toward shore in a vain bid for help—and that's where the Darwin candidate's fourth and final error became significant. He had neglected to provide his boat with the required boating safety kit, containing a fifty-foot buoyant line, an approved personal flotation device for each person on board, and a loud signaling device such as a pealess whistle.

While one's heart goes out to his wife and children, the rest of us would have seen it coming when he dived in. Although he already had several children, he certainly won't be adding any more tadpoles to the gene pool.

Reference: *Thunder Bay Chronicle-Journal*

Lifeguarding the Gene Pool

DARWIN AWARD: THE SMOKING GUN

Confirmed by Darwin

11 FEBRUARY 2001, NEW JERSEY

Two drunks were goofing around, when one challenged the
other to shoot him with cigarette butts "to see what it would feel
like." His friend obligingly loaded an antique rifle with cigarette
butts, placing black powder behind the butts to make sure they
left the barrel of the gun. He then shot his friend from a distance
of seven feet. The projectiles penetrated the ribcage of the thirty-
one-year-old who had issued the challenge, and he died of three
cigarette butts to the heart.

The gene pool is in trouble!

Reference: WMAD FM 92.1 Madison, Wisconsin,
ABC News, The Associated Press

Ironically, this story happened in a town with
the same name as an unfiltered British cigarette,
and the shooter was nicknamed "Smokey."
Too weird to believe? Confirming details:
www.Darwinawards.com/book/cigarette.html

Reader Comments:
"More ammunition in the antismoking campaign."
"Cigarettes are bad for your health."
"It's true—Smoking Kills."

DARWIN AWARD: LIBRARY RETURN

Confirmed by Darwin

11 OCTOBER 2001, TENNESSEE

Is more education the answer?

Eight freshman college students were hanging around a vacant library late one night, when they decided it would be a thrill to leap into a small opening they thought was a laundry chute.

Perhaps a few more years of college would have led them to the realization that libraries don't have laundry chutes. It was actually a trash chute feeding directly into an automatic compactor. Nineteen-year-old Wesley "Crusher" was the first to jump. He enjoyed an exhilarating three-story slide before being crushed to death in the rubbish bin below.

The other students decided not to follow.

Reference: Nashville WTVF NewsChannel5, NewsChannel9,
Nashville Tennesseean

DARWIN AWARD: CACTUS CRUNCH

Unconfirmed by Darwin

FEBRUARY 1982, ARIZONA

Desert marksmen aim their weapons at saguaro cacti so frequently that Arizona was forced to declare the "sport" a felony. Offenders risk a $100,000 fine and three years in prison. But that doesn't stop sharpshooters like twenty-seven-year-old Kenneth, who was trying to impress friends when he opened fire on a saguaro in 1982.

He was killed when it fell on him.

He reportedly fired two shells from a 16-gauge shotgun at a twenty-seven-foot cactus and began to shout, "Timber!" He only had enough time to utter the first syllable before a twenty-three-foot section of the prickly plant fell and crushed him beneath its spiky skin.

Reference: *Arizona Republic, High Country News*

Reader Comments:
"Natural gun control."
"Guess he was stuck in the desert."

DARWIN AWARD: WELL TRAINED

Confirmed by Darwin

21 MARCH 2002, KENTUCKY

In his childhood the man had whiled away many an afternoon hopping trains and riding them fifteen or twenty yards down the rails before leaping back off. But by the time he was twenty years old, he had apparently lost the knack. While demonstrating the trick to friends, our hero tried to hop a southbound train, but failed to notice the simultaneous approach of a northbound train, and was struck and killed.

Reference: Associated Press, *Louisville Courier-Journal*

Authorities are at a loss as to how to prevent train deaths. Long Island, New York, locomotive engineers recently formed a support group, as every veteran of at least a year of service has, without exception, involuntarily killed someone in a grade-crossing collision. The baffled engineers wonder how anyone could be so unaware of the laws of physics, which dictate that a fast-moving train weighing hundreds of tons has too much inertia to stop on a dime—or even a football field.

DARWIN AWARD: ROADKILL

Confirmed by Darwin
12 OCTOBER 2001, FINLAND

A group of friends was stranded beside the freeway when their automobile ran out of gas. The weather was terrible, and despite their frantic efforts, nobody would stop to help them. Eventually one member of the group became so frustrated that he stomped to the middle of the freeway and sprawled out across the road.

His friends tried to get him to move, but he yelled back, "I could sleep here!" Indeed he could. He was permanently lulled to sleep by an Audi sports car that hit and dragged him sixty yards to his death.

The police found several empty beer bottles lying around the car. We can only hope the twenty-one-year-old was drunk enough to dull the pain of the impact.

Reference: *Iltalehti, Ilta-Sanomat*

DARWIN AWARD: BLOWHOLE

Confirmed by Darwin
30 JUNE 2002, HAWAII

Eighteen-year-old Daniel was vacationing with his family when he met up with three young women on a Hawaiian beach. Perhaps the company of the lovely ladies addled his brain. Half an hour after meeting them he was frolicking in a dangerous natural waterspout called the Halona Blowhole: a rock funnel formation that shoots seawater twenty feet into the air.

A locked gate keeps people away from the stairs to the blowhole, and a warning sign proclaims Hazardous Conditions. Do Not Go Beyond This Point. A local comedian has placed a skull labeled Boneyard Reef on the warning sign. However, the area can be reached by climbing the rocks from beaches on either side, and perhaps the warning signs are not apparent.

Witnesses said that Daniel walked right by them on his way to the blowhole, and they warned him to stay away. But he kept going, climbing over the rocky shelves to reach the lava tube shortly before 3:00 P.M. He was overheard to say he wanted to feel the water hit his chest.

Thirty seconds later his wish was granted. Dozens of people watched in amazement from a highway overlook while he straddled the blowhole, arms outstretched, laughing while spray washed over him. Then a large wave hit the rocks, and a blast of water launched him five feet into the air and dropped him head-first down the blowhole.

According to a firefighter, who searched the crevice while tied to a safety rope, the blowhole narrows then opens up eight feet down. "You could tell when a wave was coming in. There was a kind of humming sound."

Divers recovered Daniel's body the next day. It was the fourth time a victim had been swept into the blowhole since 1927. Two men died in 1969 and 1986, and one man survived in 1967. "I can't understand the mindset," said Fire Chief James Arciero.

Daniel's female companions were seen being comforted by a young man wearing a T-shirt that read, Every Day, Death Is Near.

Reference: *Honolulu Advertiser, Honolulu Star-Bulletin*

> The bereaved family filed a lawsuit against the city of Honolulu and state of Hawaii, claiming they were negligent in not posting warning signs. But the evidence presented by Hawaii newspapers tends to support the notion that "safety measures are only as good as the personal responsibility exercised by those who use the oceans."

DARWIN AWARD: FUZZY FIGHTS BACK

Unconfirmed by Darwin

1997, THE NETHERLANDS

Pekka, a forty-one-year-old visitor strolling through an Amsterdam zoo, eventually found himself in front of the bear exhibit. A bystander remembers Pekka asking whether the bear was a male or female. Nobody knew, so Pekka decided to find out for himself.

He climbed over the seven-foot fence and jumped into the enclosure. Despite urgent calls from the crowd Pekka approached the bear in question. The 390-pound adult was quietly occupied with a ball and unaware of the intruder. Amazingly, Pekka was able to take an unobtrusive peek under the hood. Still perplexed, Pekka tried to determine the animal's sex experimentally by delivering a good, hard kick between its legs.

Our friend Fuzzy turned out to be a male and responded to the assault in a typical male-bear fashion. He roared in pain and charged toward Pekka, who attempted to defend himself with a hasty karate kick in the general direction of the bear while he ran for the fence. This brilliant defense tactic failed completely, and Fuzzy proceeded to occupy the next few minutes mauling the "Bear Ball Buster."

Zookeepers arrived promptly, but not promptly enough to save the life of the ill-fated Pekka. Several rounds of tranquilizer darts later the subdued bear was taken to the on-site veterinarian. Pekka was, of course, pronounced dead at the scene.

An autopsy shed no light on the reason for Pekka's actions. There were no drugs or alcohol in his system, and his family reported that he was not suicidal, nor did they know of any mental defects other than "an exaggerated sense of bravado."

Apart from a pair of badly swollen testicles the bear was uninjured. At the time of the article zoo officials had not yet decided Fuzzy's fate.

Evolution: The lean, mean gene machine

HONORABLE MENTION: BEER CHASER

Confirmed by Darwin
15 OCTOBER 2002, TEXAS

Was the beer half full, or the brain half empty?

A man chasing a half-full beer can across a Houston freeway was hit by a Chevy truck before he could retrieve his prize. He was taken to a nearby hospital, where he was listed in critical condition.

Reference: ABC News 13 KTRK Houston

Stand back, folks. Evolution in progress!

HONORABLE MENTION: SHARK PETTING ZOO
Confirmed by Darwin
23 JULY 2001, AUSTRALIA

Hungry Shark + Stupid Humans = Full Shark + Dead Humans

The carcass of a dead whale attracted more than a feeding frenzy of hungry sharks. Local boat operators also took advantage of the macabre spectacle, and ferried dozens of paying customers to the floating feast near Cape Jervis, one hundred kilometers south of Adelaide.

As great white sharks ripped hunks of flesh from the gigantic dead mammal, curious spectators took leave of their senses and reached into the water to pet their snouts. Some even climbed onto the back of the floating meal, one carrying his child for a closer look at the feeding frenzy!

People are already forbidden from approaching living whales. Authorities are considering extending the hundred-meter exclusion zone to dead whales.

"These creatures are not toys," said Environment Minister Iain Evans. "I am shocked at [their] disrespect for their own safety." He added that the government would "look at changing the law in order to protect people too stupid to protect themselves."

Marine officials say the southern right whale died from natural causes.

Reference: ananova.com, Reuters, CNN

Do we need "Jaws Laws"? A ban on approaching dead whales is ill advised, not (only) because it saves the stupid, but because it prohibits more cautious gawkers from closely observing the fascinating spectacle of a shark feeding frenzy. There's nothing dangerous about watching such a scene from a large boat—if you remember to keep your limbs well away from the gaping maws of these predators.

Natural laws have no pity.
—Robert Heinlein

HONORABLE MENTION: STUDENT FILM FOLLY

Confirmed by Darwin

19 FEBRUARY 2001, IRELAND

Teenagers in Northern Ireland ran into trouble while filming a video about the stupid risks students take. They decided that it would be a waste of a good opportunity if they were to film the documentary without actually taking those risks.

The teenagers, therefore, were filming themselves jumping from a cliff into the sea when a swell swept eleven of them into the ocean. Seven managed to swim to safety, and the remaining four were rescued in the nick of time by lifeboat. The captain said the amateur filmmakers were lucky to be alive.

Reference: BBC News

HONORABLE MENTION: TWICE THE PAIN
Unconfirmed by Darwin
3 AUGUST 2001, PENNSYLVANIA

A Philadelphia resident, wondered what it felt like to be hit by a bullet. Not one to sit idle with his curiosity unsated, he picked up a gun and shot himself in the shoulder. He was transported to the hospital by ambulance and treated for his self-inflicted injury.

Not long after his recovery he shot himself again, and the ambulance was summoned a second time. Why did he shoot himself twice? In his own words, "I wanted to see if it hurt as much as it did the first time."

Reference: *Bizarre News*

Live and learn. Or you won't live long.

PERSONAL ACCOUNT: RECTUM NEARLY KILLED'M
JUNE 2000

More common than you might think!

As a nurse in the intensive care unit of a large medical center, I've had the opportunity to care for many potential recipients of the Darwin Award. The man in this story didn't lose his life but lost his dignity and claim to common sense, among other injuries.

A middle-aged man complained of abdominal pain and rectal bleeding. He claimed to be unaware of any reason he should be presenting such symptoms, but during his examination the physician discovered a coat hanger protruding from the patient's rectum.

The charge nurse called us to announce a patient coming from the ER who had undergone an emergency bowel resection. My coworkers and I speculated about possible reasons someone might require emergency bowel surgery, until finally, the phone rang again. We sat in rapt silence while the report nurse filled us in on the details of this unfortunate soul's plight.

The man, when questioned, admitted he had inflicted the injury upon himself.

Earlier that night, while his wife was at work, he was "pleasuring himself" when he impulsively pushed an uncooked egg into his anus. When he "lost it up there," he panicked, and tried to fish it out with a coat hanger.

The coat hanger became snagged.

At this point he decided that the vibration from a motorcycle ride might dislodge the whole mess from his nether region. It did not.

Finally, in growing pain, he rode his motorcycle to the ER.

The physician removed the coat hanger and repaired his intestines.

After an hour, the man's wife arrived. Minutes later, she stormed out of his room and demanded to be informed what had happened. I told her she needed to discuss that with her husband. "He said he didn't know!" she answered. "He said the medical staff wouldn't tell him anything!"

She was politely, but firmly, instructed to speak to the man's physician.

Reference: Anonymous Personal Account

**It's only funny until someone gets hurt . . .
then it's hilarious!**

Personal Account: Repeat Offender
2002

I recently created three opportunities to remove myself from the gene pool. God must have appreciated the humor I provided that day, as I was allowed to survive to share my experience with others.

(1) While working on the electrical system in my basement, I decided to remove an outlet without shutting down the circuit. I began unscrewing the outlet with my hand on the shaft of the screwdriver. The screwdriver slipped and jammed into the main wires, sending 120-volt vibes through my body. Fortunately, my convulsions jerked me free, but I stumbled into a tool shelf and power saws, drills, and other heavy objects rained down on me.

(2) Scraped, bruised, and stunned, I collected my wits and decided I had been wrong to neglect shutting off the circuit. The fuse box was located in the ceiling, of all places. I climbed a step stool beneath it, reached up with one hand, and released the safety catch. The five-pound wooden door swung down and smacked me in the face, breaking my nose and knocking me off the ladder and onto the concrete floor.

(3) Now I was mad. I grabbed the nearest object, a crescent wrench, and whipped it at the fuse box. It ricocheted from the fuse-box door to the basement window, shattering the window and sending shards of glass everywhere. Still stunned from the blow from the fuse-box hatch, I walked barefoot across the floor. . . .

After bandaging my feet, cleaning various scrapes and wounds, and staunching the blood flow from my nose, I called it a day.

Reference: Anonymous Personal Account

PERSONAL ACCOUNT: WAG THE DOG
2002

A friend of mine was stepping out of the shower one day when his wife's small dog wandered into the bathroom. My friend loves to tease this dog, and having nothing better at hand with which to tease, he grabbed his penis and began waving it at the dog.

The dog leapt up and caught the offending member in its mouth and held on for a moment, its entire weight suspended from my friend's organ. Needless to say, this was extremely painful, and the resulting anguished scream scared the dog so badly that it let go and ran for dear life. The dog was found, much later, still hiding beneath the bed.

Did I mention that the dog had sharp teeth? Apparently they were sharp enough to go all the way through my friend's penis. Since they had punctured some well-vascularized tissue, he began to bleed profusely. Dizzy and scared, he drove himself to the emergency room.

When the nurse asked what the problem was, he tried to get away with telling her that he had a rather embarrassing injury and needed to see a doctor. Nothing doing! The nurse assured him that she had heard everything, and he must tell her exactly what had happened so she could triage him appropriately.

Once he explained the situation, she handled it quickly and professionally, putting him in a private room with only a slight smile and a stifled laugh.

After treatment and testing to ensure that nothing vital was irreparably damaged, the doctor admonished him to be more careful, and my friend made his way home to wait for his wife and explain to her how he had come to be injured. Luckily, he ended up with nothing more than an unusual scar and some painful memories, although he came damn close (well, the dog did) to eliminating any chance at contributing to the gene pool.

Reference: Anonymous Personal Account

I'm glad I didn't think of that!

PERSONAL ACCOUNT: SEXY SNACK SLAYS
MARCH 2002, COLORADO

I was a third-year medical student doing my first surgical rotation, when a man came in who had consumed, along with a copious amount of alcohol, the panties of a local stripper.

After he sobered up, he waited for the panties to pass through, but they never emerged, and he began to feel bloated. That's when the fearless fellow tried to fish them out with a hook constructed from a wire coat hanger.

The predictable result: He was not able to snag the panties but instead ripped gashes along the length of his esophagus. He died from the effects of a massive infection, removing himself from the breeding population.

His X rays were the highlight of my very first M&M (mortality and morbidity) conference. I don't think this was published, but there are other surgeons in the Denver area who remember the case.

Reference: Anonymous Personal Account

PERSONAL ACCOUNT: STAG PARTY
JUNE 2002, GEORGIA

A Georgia EMT responded to a call late one night. They arrived on the scene to find a severely injured man lying at the edge of a field. His stomach had been completely torn open, and he was covered with lacerations and bruises. He also had a prominent tire tread across his chest.

The injured man's companion showed up in a racing-model ATV (all-terrain vehicle) and, clearly intoxicated, gave the following account. Imagine this tale being recited in a deep Georgian accent.

He and his injured friend had been drinkin' and ridin' around the field on the three-wheeled ATV, when they sighted a stand of deer in their headlights. The friend, riding the back as a passenger, was struck with a great idea. "Hey, man, if you quarter off one a those deer, betcha I can bulldog'm." The driver thought this was an entertaining idea, so he proceeded to isolate a buck and race him down.

His intoxicated passenger leapt from the ATV, grabbed the buck by the antlers, and performed an excellent example of this rodeo sport. He pinned the animal's head to the ground, but that's when things went wrong. The buck, less docile than a steer, simply got up, threw his head back, and tore his assailant's belly open. The deer then proceeded to stomp, kick, and butt him for good measure.

The EMTs noticed that this information accounted for all of the injuries except one. When they asked the driver about the tire track across his injured friend's chest, he responded: "Well, how else was I s'posed to git the deer off 'im?"

I don't know which is worse: a drunk moron trying to wrestle a grown male deer like a steer, or a drunk moron who runs over his injured friend to scare away the righteously angered animal.

Reference: Anonymous Personal Account

A Wisconsin reader says, "I've observed and hunted deer in a variety of situations for years. I find it difficult to believe *anyone* on an ATV could corner one of these fleet-footed animals. A deer can duck an arrow fired from a compound bow, leap most fences, and change direction on a dime. You're not going to corner a deer unless it's tied to a post."

PERSONAL ACCOUNT: UNCLE RICK'S END
2001, COLORADO

Uncle Rick (God bless his soul) won't mind this story, as he's in a better place now.

My father and all his brothers, including Uncle Rick, the tallest, went camping at the Black Canyon of the Gunnison National Park, also known as the "Big Ninety-Degree Cliff." Back in the early seventies some campsites were placed right next to the canyon, and there were few safety warnings.

Fate had it that Dad and his brothers got one of those campsites.

They had a lot of beer that night, went to bed, and two hours later Uncle Rick woke up, still drunk, with a full bladder. Uncle Rick figured he'd pee in the canyon. Y'know, drunk guy, full tank, never urinated in a canyon before, so he walked over to the canyon and let fly.

In midstream a gust of wind came along and upset drunken Uncle Rick's equilibrium. He lost his balance and toppled over, and they found him the next day, fifty vertical feet and five horizontal feet from where he last whizzed.

I nominate Uncle Rick for a Darwin Award because I just want him to be famous for something better than being the dead guy in the family. Please forgive me, Uncle Rick.

Reference: Anonymous Personal Account

Perhaps this story should be disqualified, as people have a reasonable expectation of not stumbling into a bottomless crevasse yards away from their sleeping bags. On the other hand, they knew they were camping next to the Black Canyon and presumably were aware of the vertical drop-off when they set up camp.

Selection? Naturally!

CHAPTER 3

Explosions:
Short Sharp Shock

*James Watson, codiscoverer of the helical structure
of DNA, on correcting stupidity with gene therapy:
"If you're really stupid, I would call that a disease.
I'd like to get rid of [stupidity]."*

—*New Scientist*, February 28, 2003

The destructive nature of fire and explosives has long
been a lure for the more adventurous among us. But
a fascination with all things flammable can lead to
trouble, as shown by these eyebrow-searing tales of
grenades, gelignite, bombs, gasoline, and flaming alcoholic desserts.

BEWARE
FALLING
NUMERALS

DISCUSSION: FLAMES

I cannot help but notice that there is no problem
between us that cannot be solved by your departure.
—Mark Twain

From the subtle to the confrontational the Darwin Awards have received a panoply of criticisms from people who share an amusing tendency toward irrationality. Why bash the Darwin Awards? There are three main reasons: Some think death is too macabre to be funny. Others think that evolution is a ridiculous notion. And a small subset find it amusing . . . until they read a story about a friend.

The flames have had a beneficial effect on the Darwin Awards. For instance, a story that gets a large number of flames will receive more careful scrutiny, which means that the selections overall are more amusing to a wider audience. A story that is highly criticized on its technical merits may well be deemed fictitious. And disagreements over the qualities necessary for a "real" Darwin Award winner led to the creation of the rules, described on pages 4–9.

Here is a collection of humorous and sometimes constructive criticisms leveled against the Darwin Awards.

Eloquent Flames

It may be that Darwin Award winners epitomize the best of human nature, rather than the worst. As one thoughtful writer mused, "Can one truly distinguish lunacy from brilliance? Where would humankind be without the input of the Wright brothers, the Henry Fords, the Beethovens? The loss of man's ability to imagine, to dream, and to experiment would leave us living huddled in caves, worshiping lightning and chewing roots. As funny and bizarre as they seem, the Darwin Awards winners represent the greatness of humanity. Without the foolish idealism of the human imagination we would never have eaten oysters, bungee jumped, or reached for the stars."

Another fan complained about a not-in-my-backyard attitude prevalent among detractors. "I find it remarkable that some readers find tragedy awful when it happens in the United States but funny when it happens in South America. People do stupid things and pay with their lives, the world over. Let's enjoy it wherever it happens." Oddly enough, there are cultural differences in the way different peoples perceive the humor value of a story set in their own country, as opposed to someone else's. For example, Americans most appreciate stories about *American* winners, while Germans prefer stories about *non-German* winners.

When flames are published on the website, intrigued readers sometimes write to ask where to find the story. "This story is sick, vile, and probably really funny, and I don't know where to find it on your website. Please help me laugh at an innocent person!"

There was a memorable flame from a reader who belatedly remembered to support free speech. The first message read, "It is reprehensible to make light of the tragedy of a person losing his life. I am appalled and deeply offended. You should be ashamed of yourself. Do us a favor and remove yourself from the gene pool!" In her next email she was a bit calmer. "I must apologize for the letter I sent earlier. It was rude and uncalled for. I was offended by your website and won't visit it again, but please disregard my other comments."

Occasionally a reader with peculiar views expresses distaste for what he regards as Charles Darwin's lamentable contribution to science. "I couldn't help but laugh in disbelief when I figured it out what this is about. I don't mean to be rude, but the Darwinian mythology has been obliterated by modern science. How is it that people still stand by Darwin's racist, sexist philosophies?" Another reader's rebuttal: "Charles Darwin was a brilliant man who spent twenty-five years trying to reconcile his devout religious views with his findings before publishing. I am offended by people like you who accuse him of moral lapses."

Particularly ironic flames come from readers who have previously enjoyed the Darwin Awards but turn against them when a friend or family member becomes eligible. One woman said she was reading the Darwin Awards on an airplane and immensely enjoying the stories . . . until she was shocked to find her uncle in the book. She went on to lambaste the Darwin Awards for making fun of a kind, loving man. This turn-on-a-dime approach to humor happens on an infrequent but regular basis. Such flames prompt the self-evident observation that if you yourself are not willing to be nominated, should the circumstances of your lamentable demise merit it, you probably should NOT be reading the Darwin Awards!

By far the majority of flames, however, are less articulate than those presented above. "I find it disturbing that you would represent such nonsense. Your Award should go to yourselves, because in my opinion you are dumb!"

Transient Flames

I often converse with those who flame a specific story. Because if I've made a mistake in judgment, I want to correct it. In Chapter 6 I discuss a number of disqualified nominations. Sometimes these dialogues end with the disgruntled complainer reversing her opinion, as happened in the following correspondence.

"I was perturbed by seeing a Darwin Award published so soon after the event. I know that it is your business—hell, I've been laughing at your stories for years now—but that incident was a tragedy to the town and all who knew Ana. One could only pity [her family] for having their daughter taken in such a traumatic way."

I replied, "Wow, you've been laughing at my stories for years, but this one isn't funny. Do you think it's because it's too close to home, or is it actually not a good example of self-inflicted accidental death? I don't want to keep stories that aren't true contenders. Thanks for letting me know how you feel about this story."

The writer replied, "No, no, you're right of course, Darwin. Perhaps I was feeling a bit sensitive to it that day. As you say, perhaps it was a bit close to home, as I had seen the family interviewed on TV and felt [compassion] for them. It was a stu-

pid way to die, and Ana has every right to be on your site. Thanks for the reply. I will continue to enjoy your wit."

Read about Ana's "trashy" death.
www.DarwinAwards.com/book/ana.html

And of course there are also many cheerful fans who make it all worthwhile. "Somehow the stories make me feel, well, normal. My son is the family herpetologist, and we have twenty-one snakes in our basement. Does this make me a candidate for a Darwin Award?"

Fame is fleeting, but dumb is forever

Darwin Award: Blown Away

Confirmed by Darwin
16 July 2001, Mississippi

An assistant plant manager for Blacklidge Emulsions died when he used an acetylene torch to cut a hole in a ten-thousand-gallon tank of asphalt emulsion. He was attempting to visually survey the amount of emulsion that remained in the tank, but according to an OSHA representative, "no safety precautions were taken before the cutting operation began. [His] attention was twice called to a warning sign on the side of the structure which stated the contents were combustible. In complete disregard of safety procedures" the erstwhile manager lit an acetylene torch and began cutting, causing an explosion that blew him ninety-three feet away.

Reference: *CCH Employment Safety & Health Guide,* Issue 1573,
OSHA Regional News Release, *Biloxi Sun Herald*

Reader Comments:
"One less administrator? Survival of the species at its best!"
"That's what I call 'having a blow.' "
"Managers are NOT immune!"
"<long sigh>"

Never underestimate the power of human stupidity.
—Robert Heinlein

DARWIN AWARD: WRONG AND WRONGER

Unconfirmed by Darwin

29 JULY 2002, UKRAINE

Late one night the inhabitants of Yuvieyna village, a suburb of Luhansk, awoke to a loud explosion. Not long before the explosion a forty-year-old deputy of the local administration board had taken his dog out for a walk. He encountered a police academy cadet who was escorting two women to their homes.

The cadet pointed out that the deputy's dog was not allowed on a public street without a lead and muzzle. Now, only an exceedingly bold cadet would be presumptuous enough to tell a village deputy what to do, so the two men began to argue. Unable to resolve the matter by verbal means, the deputy finally pulled out a military RGD-5 hand grenade and threw it to the cadet's feet. His well-trained dog immediately ran for the object and fetched it for his master . . . and man and dog met the same messy fate.

Police are investigating how the deputy came to have a grenade in a country where citizens are forbidden to carry arms, let alone military ordnance.

Reference: 1+1 TV Channel Ukraine

DARWIN AWARD: ROCKET TESTER
Confirmed by Darwin
8 JUNE 1983, NORTH CAROLINA

The army base at Fort Bragg has seen its share of military "accidents," including the following, a true story and an object lesson often recounted on explosive device ranges to teach soldiers a basic safety lesson: LEAVE A DUD ROUND WHERE IT LIES.

At the LAW (light antitank weapon) range, soldiers are afforded the rare privilege of firing a real LAW round, although the test rounds are smaller and not armed with the full explosive power of the actual LAWs. They have an orange chalk warhead and resemble a model rocket.

One day the designated Range Safety Officer, Sergeant Lowe, was assigned the job of setting up the moving target with the assistance of a three-man detail. "The installation of the target on the carrier was hampered by the absence of proper tools," so they improvised and used a steel tent peg as a hammer to nail the target to the carrier.

While walking on the firing range Sergeant Lowe spotted and picked up an M72A2 66mm LAW dud round that had not exploded upon impact with the target. The other men in the detail warned him to leave it on the ground and let the EOD (explosive ordinance detachment) handle it. Sergeant Lowe replied, "It's just an old dud," and, to illustrate the innocuous nature of the round, began to strike it with the steel tent peg.

The second strike tripped the pressure-sensitive piezoelectric detonator, causing the round to explode. The explosion tore off Sergeant Lowe's left arm, parts of his right hand, and inflicted fatal wounds to his lungs and abdominal area.

Instead of the EOD a medical evacuation aircraft was dispatched from the hospital, and an army forensics team arrived to literally scoop up the remains of the former "Range Safety Officer."

Always remember, LEAVE A DUD ROUND WHERE IT LIES!

Reference: *U.S. Army Safety Incidents and Reports* #19830608001

Foolproof systems do not take into account the ingenuity of fools

DARWIN AWARD: SAW A GRENADE

Unconfirmed by Darwin
JULY 2002, GERMANY

This story was told at a symposium dinner by two Austrian pathologists. A deceased male was brought to them for a post-mortem. He had suffered severe head trauma. According to police reports the man had wanted to see how a German World War II hand grenade was constructed. His curiosity led him to clamp the grenade in a vise and cut a thin band around the center with a circular saw, so that he would be able to crack open the two halves. Unfortunately, the man cut a little too deeply, and detonated the grenade. The pathologists stated that the man had very little brain material when he was brought to them; however, they were not sure if that was a result of the explosion!

JANUARY 2002, CROATIA
Confirmed by Darwin

In a similar mishap, a Croatian was killed while trying to open a hand grenade with a chain saw. He wanted to retrieve the explosive to make firecrackers for the New Year's holiday. At least he went out with a bang!

DARWIN AWARD: FIR KILLS TREE TRIMMER
Confirmed by Darwin
15 JUNE 2002, ENGLAND

A safety harness doesn't always help.

A tree surgeon decided to save time and throw the pruned branches directly into a fire he built near the base of the tree. He was perched high in a fir tree, lopping branches and tossing them in the fire, when one of the branches became propped against the trunk. The tree caught fire, putting an end to any further time-saving innovations.

Reference: BBC News

Death by Natural Selection

ZEEBARF '03

HONORABLE MENTION: SHELL NECKLACE

Unconfirmed by Darwin
10 MARCH 2001, WASHINGTON

A nineteen-year-old Spokane man attempted to string a neck-lace of live ammunition. He was punching holes in the shell casings using an awl and hammer, when one of the projectiles exploded, damaging his hand and teaching him that he should have collected his shells from the beach instead of the artillery range.

Gene Pool Reject

HONORABLE MENTION: WET 'N' DRY SHOP VAC
Confirmed by Darwin
15 OCTOBER 2002, WASHINGTON

Gasoline is a dangerous substance. You're apt to win a Darwin Award if you stick a road flare in a puddle of gas, check the level in a fuel can with a cigarette lighter, or set ants ablaze with it. Now, a new way to get in trouble with gasoline has been discovered!

Firefighters summoned to a residential fire arrived to find twenty-foot flames shooting out of two Chevy Astro vans. After quelling the gasoline-fed blaze with water, dry chemicals, and foam, they questioned the man responsible for the incident.

Turns out that our Honorable Mention decided to siphon gasoline with an electric wet 'n' dry shop vac. Amazingly, he had managed to collect and transfer an entire bucketful of gasoline before an electrical spark ignited the fumes.

A safety spokesperson said, "This was an accident waiting to happen."

Reference: *King County Journal*

HONORABLE MENTION: PHENOMENAL FAILURE

Unconfirmed by Darwin

FEBRUARY 2001, MICHIGAN

A twenty-eight-year-old demolition worker attempted to commit suicide by washing down nitroglycerine pills with vodka. Normally suicide is not worthy of an Honorable Mention, but this man's failure mode was exceptional. After swallowing the pills he tried to explode the nitroglycerine by repeatedly ramming himself into a wall. He was treated for bruises and released from the hospital, after some much-needed counseling.

Reference: *Detroit Times*

**The creative answer to the question
"To be or not to be?"**

HONORABLE MENTION: PUMPED UP!

Unconfirmed by Darwin
1989, CALIFORNIA

The location: a small boat harbor in Santa Cruz. The victims: a sailboat and its owner. The opening scene: employees sprinting away from the dock's fuel pumps—a vision guaranteed to evoke dread in the souls of innocent bystanders.

If those around you are fleeing in terror, it's a good bet that you should follow in their footsteps. Within seconds the entire deck of a cabin cruiser blasted five feet out of the water, propelled by enough force to fell an elephant. A bystander outside a nearby restaurant reported seeing a man fly from the airborne deck and land in the water near the flaming vessel.

The harbor patrol was on the scene within seconds. They fished the unconscious man from the water, and then quickly hauled the burning wreck over to a boat ramp before it set the fuel dock ablaze.

It turned out that the man spotted flying through the air had just purchased the boat and was filling its tanks before he set sail to San Francisco. As he prepared to motor away from the fuel dock, a dock attendant noticed that he had pumped the fuel into a fishing-pole holder instead of his tanks!

The alarmed employee instructed him to turn on his bilge pump and blowers, but the man stated that he was in too much of a hurry to wait for the fumes to clear. As the attendant ran for his life, sparks from the engine's starter motor ignited the accumulated fumes.

The boat was dragged from the water with a bulldozer and hauled to the junkyard as scrap. The owner was alive when he was carted off by the ambulance, but one way or another, his odds of surviving long in this world seem poor.

Reference: *Santa Cruz Sentinel* and an eyewitness account.

**Help natural selection:
Eliminate warning labels!**

HONORABLE MENTION: HUNGER VERSUS FEAR
Confirmed by Darwin
8 JANUARY 2001, FLORIDA

Greed knows no bounds, even when the situation is life threatening. In an Orlando restaurant a fire spread when a rusty metal chimney ignited the old dry wood surrounding it. Flames shot from the roof and the dining area began to fill with smoke. Patrons rushed to the exits to flee the burning restaurant . . . at least, most of them did. But one greedy patron rushed to the buffet to fill his plate with food so he could eat outside, and another was seen stealing tips from the tables in the smoke-filled room. Two prime examples of people intent on removing themselves from the gene pool!

Reference: *Orlando Sentinel*

Evolution for the Hell of It

HONORABLE MENTION: BAKED ALASKA
Confirmed by Darwin
JUNE 1983, CANADA

I was the commanding officer of a seventy-five-foot navy diving tender, YST 10. Our mission was to train future naval officers to navigate the Strait of Georgia, northwest of Vancouver. It was a lovely June afternoon, with clear blue skies and gentle breezes. A trainee spotted a flicker of fire on the horizon where there should have been nothing but water. We immediately turned toward the fire and turned up the radio to listen for distress calls. As we approached, the flicker turned into a distant pillar of fire.

Then came the distress call.

Two businessmen had decided to give their wives the vacation of a lifetime, and they rented a sailboat. Their plan was to explore the marine sanctuary and watch for whales.

The previous day they had sailed from Vancouver into a stiff breeze. Both ladies got very seasick and demanded an end to the "dream" vacation. But by noon the second day the ladies had recovered, and decided that the vacation might be as wonderful as their husbands had promised.

They created a Baked Alaska to surprise, and perhaps to show forgiveness to, their husbands. Unfortunately they decided to light the Baked Alaska on the ladder to the cockpit, right under the mainsail! The flicker that turned into a pillar of flames was the sail catching fire.

They were rescued by helicopter.

We tried to salvage the yacht, but it burned and sank.

References: Eyewitness account of a Canadian navy lieutenant;
corroborated by a Canadian navy lieutenant commander,
and a personal acquaintance of the two couples.

This story is designated "confirmed" despite a lack of traditional verification, due to its plausible nature, the trustworthiness of the eyewitness, and corroboration by two independent sources. A friend of the couples involved said they were "a bit mentally scarred" and that "the likelihood of the ladies ever getting on a boat again are very slim."

A Baked Alaska is a baked meringue over ice cream, on a base of cake. A flame is sometimes used to brown the tips of the meringue—Martha Stewart uses a propane torch—but most cooks just put the dessert under the broiler.

PERSONAL ACCOUNT: FAMOUS LAST WORDS
Unconfirmed by Darwin
OCTOBER 1982

In the New Zealand army the staff was having a discipline problem with four cadets posted at Waiouru Camp. The group had been confined to barracks for a day as punishment, while the rest of the unit participated in a training activity.

The four cadets decided to abscond, and set out on a jaunt into the training area, heedless of the consequences. How bad could another day of rest be? After walking some distance they found themselves on the range used as the training grounds of the M203 grenade launcher. As they sauntered around the range, they came across several unexploded rounds.

From day one army recruits are told never to touch anything even remotely resembling unexploded ordnance. Indeed, there are signs surrounding every range the army uses, stating the rule again. It is incessantly drummed into every brain in the army. But not everyone learns. . . .

The ringleader of this group picked up two grenades and held them at arm's length, while his mates egged him on. According to the survivors he uttered those famous last words "Hey, fellas, look at this!" Words to make seasoned men duck and cover.

The cadet cracked the two grenades together, causing one or both to explode in his hands. The M203 grenade has a lethal blast area of five meters and left little for the medics to recover.

The other three miscreants were injured by shrapnel but survived to be disciplined in a far more lenient fashion than their fallen fellow.

Reference: Geoff Crowhurst, Personal Account

**Famous Last Words:
"Hey, fellas, look at this!"**

PERSONAL ACCOUNT: ACETYLENE FUN? NOT!

1993, ONTARIO, CANADA

After I borrowed a welding torch and used it cut up an old water tank on my family's property, I found myself with leftover partial bottles of oxygen and acetylene. It seemed wrong to waste all that gas, particularly since I had heard about fuel-oxygen explosives and had always wanted to test the concept.

I extinguished the torch safely by setting it to the "leanest" possible burn and smacking the tip against a flat surface. I then filled a large plastic garbage bag (thirteen gallons) with oxygen and acetylene from the torch and inserted a six-inch visco cannon fuse.

I placed the homemade explosive—words to send fear into the bravest heart—on a big rock by the river. I remember lighting the fuse, and I remember backing away as it began to burn. The next thing I knew, I returned to consciousness in the river!

Both of my eardrums were broken, and I was bleeding from both ears and my nose. My beard and exposed hair were singed and curly, but oddly, there were no burns on my skin. I later discovered a perfect image of the folds, seams, and buttons of the cotton shirt I was wearing, imprinted as bruises on my chest and arms. It took months for my eardrums to heal, and I still can't hear high frequencies well.

What happened? Perhaps a spark from the fuse touched the bag. Perhaps the bag had a small leak. Whatever the cause, I'm lucky to be alive. At the emergency room the workers said, "When we get a welder here, he usually dies."

Reference: Anonymous Personal Account

Personal Account: Backyard Body Surfing
February 2002

When I was fourteen, my fascination with fire led me to a summer-afternoon exploration of the phenomenon. First, I set fire to a wash of gasoline in my parents' driveway. This was so successful that I graduated to riding my bicycle through the flames in an emulation of Evel Knievel. The tires picked up the gasoline and flames, creating a daring visual effect. This impressed my two friends so much that they egged me on to my next death-defying stunt.

I thought I had thought the entire thing through. A pressurized garden hose stood ready for my "friends" to wield after I performed my blazing stunt of glory. Safety precaution in place, I proceeded to douse my jeans in gasoline and ignite them.

As children we are taught to stop, drop, and roll if we catch fire. However, in this case, that time-honored technique merely resulted in a flaming lawn. I suddenly realized that when I stopped moving I became extremely uncomfortable. I jumped up from the grass and commenced what my hysterical friends described as an Irish jig. Incapacitated by their guffaws, they no longer had the wherewithal to bring the garden hose to bear on my cavorting figure.

Realizing that an end to my situation was not forthcoming, my mind went into red alert. I ran for our backyard pool, an aboveground model, and leapt in. This relieved my immediate problem; however, it created an even worse one. I found myself submerged under a sheet of flaming gasoline, which began to melt the pool liner. There was nothing to do but wait it out.

I didn't have to hold my breath long, for the pool liner is an integral part of the stability of an aboveground pool. I found myself participating in a sport previously unknown in the Midwest, elsewhere referred to as "body surfing." The pool wall burst, and I completely flooded the yards of my parents and my astonished friends.

I suffered only minor burns from the fire, but the parental flames were quite another matter. The moral of the story:

Fire + Gasoline + Stupidity = $9,000 repair bill.

Reference: Anonymous Personal Account

The veracity of this tale is doubtful. Gasoline burns so hot that the boy could hardly have been expected to emerge from his pants with nothing more than "minor burns."

Personal Account: Blasting Expertise
1960s, Africa

I was working on the construction of an irrigation canal in West Africa, and it was necessary to clear the route of some extremely large trees. Gelignite was cheap and effective, and fortunately we had George on our staff to help us use it. George possessed a blasting certificate, testifying to his expertise in this field.

While he was showing an African foreman how to set up the explosives, I spotted George with a cigarette in his mouth, presumably placed there because his hands were occupied with fuse cord and sticks of gelignite. For his comfort George was seated on a fifty-six-pound case of special blasting gelatin.

Those who know explosives will realize that this situation in itself presented no problem. Gelignite may burn when ignited but will not explode unless prompted to do so by a detonator. As I walked up, I saw that George was inserting a detonator into a stick of gelignite. . . .

We all, with the exception of one tree, lived to tell the tale. However, thinking that I would not believe my own recollection of the incident unless I recorded it, I delayed running for cover until I had taken a photograph, which I have to this day. And I feel that this triumph of photography over self-preservation merits an Honorable Mention!

Reference: Peter Watts, Personal Account

Gelignite is a relatively safe explosive mixture, composed of nitroglycerin absorbed into wood pulp (or guncotton) and sodium or potassium nitrate. It was invented by Alfred Nobel, a Swedish chemist who also invented dynamite. Nobel amassed a huge fortune, which upon his death was used to fund the annual Nobel Prizes.

PERSONAL ACCOUNT: CHEMISTRY LESSON
2002, ENGLAND

I am a high school science teacher in Birmingham. I usually teach physics, but due to teacher shortages I ended up teaching chemistry a few years ago. As you are undoubtedly aware, chemistry can be fun, especially the topic of reactive metals.

I decided to liven up one particular lesson by demonstrating the awesome energy released when silver nitrate, magnesium, and a drop of water are mixed. This particular reaction is very violent, exploding in a brilliant white flash when the water is added. It usually shatters the crucible. On this particular occasion I decided to save on crockery, and put the chemicals in a sturdy mortar dish.

This was my first mistake.

I mixed the powders in the bone-dry mortar and carefully, at arm's length, added a drop of water with a pipette. A small fizz preceded a violent flash, and a collective "Ahhh!" emanated from the impressed pupils.

As always on these occasions the pupils shouted, "Do it again, sir!" As always I said, "Okay!" But this time I didn't need a new crucible, because Mr. Clever had used a sturdy, reusable mortar dish.

I proceeded to add the chemicals again to the mortar, and that was my second mistake.

I added the silver nitrate crystals and crushed them with the pestle. I then added a liberal spatula of magnesium powder and began to mix the two, my head bent over the dish. Unfortunately for me the mortar was damp and warm from the previous reaction. Fortunately for me, as well as having inherited a stupidity gene, I inherited a gene for fast reflex actions.

At the first hint of a fizz I threw my head back while simultaneously shielding the mortar from my face and body with my hands, as the violence of nature was unleashed from the chemicals in the dish. Within a hundredth of a second the reactants spewed forth their energy in a blinding flash of pure white light and heat. You can guess what happened to my hands.

My third mistake occurred later at home, after my trip to the hospital for emergency treatment. Both hands were heavily bandaged, and my head was fuzzy on account of the prescription painkillers I had taken for the excruciating pain of the second-degree burns. I decided to have a cigarette, since it had been a pretty rough day. I don't know if you've ever operated a cigarette lighter with fully bandaged hands. Let me just say I found it rather ironic that burn dressings are flammable.

To finish off, I would like to apologize to my three children. I'm sorry if you've inherited that particular gene of mine that leads me to do stupid things.

Reference: Anonymous Personal Account

Films of laboratory demonstrations:
www. DarwinAwards.com/book/chemistry.html

PERSONAL ACCOUNT: CHRISTMAS FIREWORKS
1980S

A true tale of an event from my ill-spent youth.

It was a cold, clear Christmas day, and only one gift remained unopened: a large present under the tree addressed to the entire family from Santa. My younger brothers and I were granted the honor of opening it, and we proceeded to rip the wrapping paper asunder. It was a boxful of fireworks! Bottle rockets, firecrackers, screamers, flowers, snakes, smoke bombs, and M60s, which resemble miniature sticks of dynamite.

After securing our other presents in our rooms, we threw on our new winter coats, grabbed the box of fireworks, and scouted out a location from which to deploy them. We chose the top of a hill overlooking the lake in our backyard, toward which we would launch the fireworks.

To be safe we decided to leave the box of fireworks in the garage, twenty feet from our staging ground. But after several trips back and forth I decided to carry the fireworks more efficiently. I grabbed some M60s, a string of firecrackers, and a few packages of bottle rockets, and stuffed them into the inside breast pocket of my new coat until it was close to bursting.

We were using punks to light the fuses. Punks resemble sticks of incense. They burn without a flame, leaving only a smoldering tip. I was happily engaged in lighting fireworks, when I inadvertently reached into my inside pocket for more, *with the hand holding the punk.* I did not realize my mistake until I felt a sharp burn and a powerful WHUMP against my chest.

At first I thought one of my brothers had fired a bottle rocket at me, but no one was looking my way. I suddenly realized that the bottle rocket had gone off in my inside breast pocket!

I grabbed the front collar of my coat and pulled it out so I could look down to see what was happening. Sparks flew up and hit my face. At that moment the long string of firecrackers ignited. POP! POP POP POP! I tried to unzip my coat, but it was stuck and would not unzip no matter how hard I pulled. My smoldering coat was being ripped to shreds, and holes were burning through the sweatshirt beneath it.

I realized that there was only one way to remove the coat. I whipped it over my head, and had barely extricated my arms from the sleeves and hurled it away, when the first M60 blew. I dived to the cold ground, which felt soothing against my burned chest. The M60 ripped a huge hole in the coat, which started to burn, and the burning cloth set off the rest of the M60s, blowing the coat into tatters of flaming material.

The burns on my chest were not severe. My mother, a nurse, was able to dress them herself, so I didn't have to go to the emergency room. My parents were too bemused to punish me, except for insisting that I buy myself a new coat with my Christmas money.

If the M60s had gone off while I was wearing the coat, or during my struggle to get it off, I would have been a serious contender for a Darwin Award. But since I survived, instead let my story serve as an amusing warning to others!

Reference: Justice Lloyd, Personal Account

PERSONAL ACCOUNT: FIREBUG

1994

I was fifteen, it was summer, and I had to mow the lawn. As I walked into the garage on a mission to refuel the lawn mower, I was diverted from my task by the provocative sight of ants streaming everywhere. A problem in search of a solution!

I couldn't find any bug spray, but I could find the gas can for the lawn mower. Gasoline would kill those bugs! I began to pour fuel on the ant trails. My extermination plan worked well, but the process quickly became tedious. I thought, *This is boring . . . fire is exciting . . . the garage floor is concrete . . . I won't hurt anything. . . .*

I put down the gas can and picked up the matches, and there I was, lighting my ant-killing gas puddles, selecting bigger and bigger puddles each time, when I suddenly noticed that the gas can was on fire!

I tried to kick it out of the garage, but instead it landed in the corner where Mom kept wooden tomato poles. They went up in a flash.

I grabbed the burning can and tossed it in the driveway, where the lawn mower stood waiting for me to stop killing ants and remember my chore. The lawn mower caught fire, so I shoved it down the driveway to keep it from exploding near me. By the time it blew up across the street, the fire had spread in the garage.

I was calling 911 when I heard a loud BOOM! Evidently there had been a propane tank near the late tomato poles. It certainly wasn't there anymore. I hung up the phone and grabbed the garden hose, and began fighting the flames.

By the time the fire department controlled the blaze, I had already caused $15,000 in damage to the house and garage, and suffered second-degree burns on my legs and the hand that had grabbed the burning gas can. I'm still alive by a divine miracle—and not ONCE since then have I started a conflagration.

I earned the nickname Firebug, and the ants never came back.

Reference: Anonymous Personal Account

Evidence that God is still in charge

PERSONAL ACCOUNT: FLASHY CHEF

2001

For Christmas dinner I decided to quadruple a new recipe for pepper-encrusted filet mignon. One of the ingredients was brandy, a substance I'd never cooked with before that night. The recipe called for four steaks and a cup of brandy, cooked in a ten-inch skillet. Quadrupled, the only thing that would hold the meat was a large roasting pan set over two gas burners.

In retrospect I should have realized that when four cups of brandy are poured into a roasting pan hot enough to sear meat, the resulting vapors will creep over the sides of the pan in a hurry. When these vapors ignite, the resulting fireball can, and will, remove eyebrows, nose hair, and varnish from a hapless chef's brand-new kitchen cabinets.

From now on, turkey for Christmas.

Reference: Rob McClain, Personal Account

Try the recipe yourself!
www.Drawinawards.com/book/filetmignon.html

PERSONAL ACCOUNT:
REGULAR AND EXTRA CRISPY
2001

The owner of a family entertainment center occasionally replaced out-of-date arcade and video games, and dismantled the old ones into pieces small enough to toss in the Dumpster. One day he gave a pair of intrepid game-room employees, nicknamed Podunk and Donut, after their radio call signs, the task of destroying two outmoded games.

The first game was sent to Atari heaven with no fuss, thanks to a five-pound sledgehammer. The second was more obstinate.

After the boys broke the handle of the sledgehammer against it, they decided to heave heavy cinder blocks at the machine. But that only succeeded if you consider broken cinder blocks a success. They tried ramming the game with a car, which did little but damage the vehicle's front end.

Brute force was getting them nowhere fast.

In the interest of safety, speed, efficiency, and a minimum of wear and tear on their tools, they decided to burn the game down.

Podunk filled the interior of the cabinet with fumes from an aerosol can, while Donut manned the cigarette lighter. You can guess the rest. Both employees sustained second-degree burns to their arms and faces, and the game is still alive and well.

Now the boys have new call signs: Regular and Extra Crispy.

Reference: Anonymous Personal Account

PERSONAL ACCOUNT: THE ANSWER IS . . .

2002

A young man presented himself in the emergency room covered with burns on all exposed skin. Even his hair was singed close to his scalp. What had caused these injuries? He had posed himself a question, and then, overwhelmed by curiosity, empirically determined the answer.

My colleagues in the hospital vividly remember this patient. At best he earns an Honorable Mention, since he did not die, nor did he lose his reproductive capacity.

In order to discover the answer to his question, which will soon be revealed, he proceeded to shoot a propane tank with a .22 caliber rifle. Having survived the first stage of his stupidity, he gave the propane ten minutes to leak out, and then held a burning lighter and walked slowly toward the hissing tank.

The question: How close do you have to be to the propane tank before it blows up?

The answer: Fifteen feet.

Reference: Reed Brozen, Personal Account

PERSONAL ACCOUNT: THE BARBECUED CHEF
AUGUST 2002, ONTARIO, CANADA

I was attempting to light my new barbecue lighter—a long stick with a click button—when I discovered it was out of fluid. I took the lighter to the laundry room and filled it over the sink. I later discovered that I was using the wrong type of fluid, but that's part of another story.

I decided to test it, figuring the flame would be at least eight inches from any fuel on my hand. What I hadn't counted on was the effect of the flame on the stream of fuel leaking down to the tip of the lighter. When I clicked the button, to my astonishment my whole hand caught on fire.

I hollered, "Oh, darn!" (Or words to that effect.) Having one's hand on fire is neither relaxing nor calming, and I must have flinched, thereby squeezing more fuel from the container in my other hand, engulfing my already-burning hand in a ball of flames.

At this point I dropped everything into the sink, igniting the whole shebang: the lighter, the canister of fuel, and some dust mites. Again I exclaimed, "Oh, darn!" and I began to become quite concerned.

I tried to smother the flames on my hand by clapping but just lit the other hand on fire too. I hit the floor and tried the standard stop, drop, and roll technique, but that doesn't work well on a concrete floor. I eventually extinguished my hands with a nearby floor mat, thereby leaving them free to deal with a growing concern. . . .

The laundry sink was completely engulfed in flames. I was trapped by indecision. Should I run for a gigantic box of baking soda, or would water put it out? That's when I made the worst decision of the day.

I cranked on the water taps over the basin.

Lighter fluid and water do not, in fact, mix. Now I had fast-moving liquid flames to deal with! Luckily, it turned out that turning the taps on full allowed the water to "outnumber" the fire, which was eventually put out.

At that point I made the smartest decision of all. After those thirty seconds of excitement were over, I took off my wedding ring. This served two purposes: It did not get stuck to my finger while it swelled and blistered, and it kept the world from knowing that my wife had actually married such an idiot!

And now to share with you an important safety tip I learned during this experience: When you do catch on fire, don't yell, "Oh, darn!" Instead, yell, "Fire!!! HOLY S**T, I'm f**king on fire!!!" This sends a clear message to your wife that all is not well.

Reference: Andrew Butler, Personal Account

PERSONAL ACCOUNT: GOT A MATCH?
JANUARY 2001

In 1994 I was a volunteer firefighter with a fair amount of training and experience under my belt, but not a lot of smarts under my cap. We lived in the country and had a "burning barrel" to dispose of our rubbish. It had rained a few days before, and now our barrel contained wet cardboard. I knew that wouldn't burn, so I got my jerry can and poured gas into the barrel. Not a lot, mind you, but apparently just enough.

As luck would have it my match didn't light, so I ran back into the house to get some more, while the fumes rose from the burning barrel. I returned and stood eight feet back from the barrel and threw a match. Did I mention my wife was standing beside me?

The resulting explosion actually made her long hair look like she had been riding a motorcycle at seventy miles an hour with no helmet. I burned my eyebrows and hair, and the explosion was heard down at the golf course a quarter mile away. There were small fires burning everywhere, and all I could do was stand there staring at my wife with my jaw hanging down.

Neither of us could hear a thing, as our ears were ringing to beat the band. We put out the fires with a garden hose and spent the rest of the night assuring neighbors that we had not dynamited our property.

I may amaze other people but mostly I amaze myself.

Reference: Anonymous Personal Account

Personal Account: Scrambled Eggs
2002

When I was seventeen, I pruned the future of my own family tree.

Some friends and I had heard that you can make a plastic two-liter bottle explode by using dry ice and water to create pressure inside the capped bottle. We gathered up as many plastic soda bottles as we could, obtained dry ice from the icehouse, and selected targets for this particular brand of mayhem.

After watching the first "dry ice bomb" go off, we were left disappointed with the length of time it took to build up enough pressure to actually blow. Our first idea was to use a smaller bottle, but a one-liter bottle only created a weaker, but still painfully delayed, explosion. The second idea was to use warm water to drive a faster reaction with the dry ice. This created a more reasonable time lag before the sweet satisfaction of being a successful teenage vandal came to fruition.

Now we became greedy. If warm water made it better, then hot water must make it better still! Yours truly was the one to try it. I added ice, poured scalding hot water into the bottle, and capped the "bomb." I recall an immediate ringing in my ears, and blood, and plastic shards. The hospital was only a mile away, but it seemed like a light-year.

At the hospital I was rushed in and quickly assessed. Due to the way I had been cradling the bottle, my groin and thighs took most of the damage from plastic shrapnel. At the age of thirty I have many scars to remind me of my teenage stupidity, but none as monumental as my pair of silicone testes!

Reference: Anonymous Personal Account

PERSONAL ACCOUNT: FLEAS OF FIRE
1985, THE NETHERLANDS

Hans was a single man living on the top floor of a three-story block of flats. He was trained in welding, a job requiring knowledge of flammable and compressed gases, which makes this story all the more remarkable.

Hans volunteered to provide a temporary home for his sister's cat and, unbeknownst to him, the cat's entourage of fleas. After the cat departed, the fleas remained and began to drive Hans crazy. He asked for advice and was told to treat the apartment with flea spray.

But some people are resistant to taking good advice. Hans was apparently one of these people. Instead of flea spray he chose a more drastic approach and bought ten cans of fly spray. He sealed off all the windows and doors, using duct tape, and proceeded to puncture all ten cans and leave the building while they spewed their pressurized contents.

The vapors crept toward the pilot light, which obligingly ignited the flammable mix. The result was a giant explosion that removed his apartment from the building and caused over a million guilders of damage to the neighboring flats. Glass was thrown far and wide, and cars were destroyed by flying debris.

The big winners were the fleas, which were not only unharmed by the gas and the blast but were also spread onto all the neighboring cats and dogs. Once the flea situation became known, his neighbors offered to help make Hans a Darwin Award winner by removing him and his genes from circulation, but as far as we know, only his reputation was harmed.

Reference: Andrea Mica, Personal Account

PERSONAL ACCOUNT: THEORETICAL KNOWLEDGE
APRIL 1998, CANADA

I emerged from my high school chemistry class, not my best subject, and was on the way to the cafeteria when I was joined by Mr. Junior Einstein, who was happily spouting chemical gibberish. Have you ever noticed that some people talk smart but act like future Darwin Award winners?

Einstein began pontificating on reactions caused by adding heat to certain elements such as neon and aluminum. When we reached the cafeteria, he nonchalantly placed his food in the microwave oven. As it cooked, he explained that aluminum can explode when heated sufficiently. As he talked, I began to detect the faint scent of smoke in the air, which I mentioned to my guest lecturer.

As we turned toward the microwave, Einstein's jaw dropped low enough to accommodate a rack of test tubes. His dish of food was blazing. One second later the oven was rocked by a loud KABLAAM!

This candidate for an Honorable Mention suddenly discovered that theoretical knowledge does not equal practical wisdom. The chemistry lesson he learned in the cafeteria was far more valuable: "Don't mix aluminum foil with heat!"

Reference: Anonymous Personal Account

CHAPTER 4

Women: Female Finale

Common sense is . . . the most equally divided,
but surely the most underemployed,
talent in the world.

—Christine Collange

Our mothers warned us, "Don't run with scissors!"
But they never warned us about shaving before a wet
T-shirt contest, petting hippopotami and lion cubs,
and other activities temporarily enjoyed by the fol-
lowing damsels in distress.

DISCUSSION: VICIOUS KILLER MEMES

Throughout our lives we learn to adapt to our surroundings, including our social environment. Since the advent of agriculture humans have been congregating in increasingly large groups. Today's dense urban populations are made possible, not by genetic changes, but by cultural adaptations that allow us to coexist in large communities.

For instance, the shared belief that we should obey traffic signals and road conventions makes safe driving possible. If 10 percent of drivers were unwilling to stop at red lights, if 1 percent of drivers drove on the wrong side of the road, if even one driver in a thousand enjoyed ramming into fellow commuters, driving would be considered an extreme sport rather than standard transportation. But most people don't swerve unannounced into our lanes, do brake for pedestrians, and even avoid parking in handicapped spots. We expect the person walking in front of us to hold open the door if our arms are full of heavy packages, and in turn, we hold the door for others. We speak our opinions in conversation and remember to shut up so that others can have their say. Jointly held social conventions work for the good of all.

A cohesive community confers great benefits on all, but for that community to exist a majority of people must follow the conventions. Queues are a good illustration of this principle. In some cultures people form a line to reach a limited resource. People who stand in line rely on newcomers to voluntarily stand behind them. The newcomer, however, would benefit from "cutting the line" near the front of the queue. What stops him? If too many people cheat, the alternative would be to cluster around the resource so that a newcomer would be unable to "cut." On average the benefit of mutually agreeing to queue outweighs the downside of forming a disorganized cluster, and so the shared convention of the queue is born.

Because a single individual who breaks rules can otherwise reap personal benefits at the cost of community cohesion, there are social and legal sanctions against rule breakers. Line cutters are awarded public disapproval, a conditioning that begins in grammar school. Chronic convention-flouters are considered rude, and because we don't like them or trust them, they are less likely to be granted the benefits of a shared community. Ostracism, an extreme form of social reprisal, is a powerful tool to control individual behavior, as are laws that directly impact a rule breaker's property and freedom.

A meme is a unit of cultural information. While most social memes work in a protective, functional manner, some are dysfunctional. One example is intolerance toward those whose beliefs differ from one's own. Such intolerance may act as a cohesive force in a small, closed community, but one can no longer avoid rubbing elbows with people whose beliefs are dramatically different, and it is necessary to coexist peacefully with them. Another example is the notion that hard work is more important than education. This idea is adequate for a community that needs more elbow grease than diplomas, but in our current society, rich in information and full of labor-

saving devices, social groups who discount the importance of education are becoming increasingly marginalized.

Some memes are not only dysfunctional, they are downright destructive. For instance, when driving at night, one commonly flashes one's headlights at a car driving unsafely without its headlights on. A few years ago a rumor spread over the Internet that gang members intending to kill a random person were selecting their victims by driving without lights after dark and targeting those who flashed their headlights. The idea that one might be murdered for performing a good deed is particularly unpleasant, because it's an example of a vicious killer meme destroying a previously helpful meme.

> **For more information about the dramatic effects of cultural memes, read Jared Diamond's treatise of human history** *Guns, Germs and Steel,* **and Deborah Tannen's classic communication book** *That's Not What I Meant.*

The Darwin Awards play a small role in creating and reinforcing beneficial memes. In the stories that follow, you will be reminded that gasoline is not a cure for head lice, that caged lions are dangerous, that driving amid distractions on a windy mountainous road is not a good idea, and that unlicensed plastic surgeons are bad news for bored housewives.

DARWIN AWARD: BASS ACKWARDS

Unconfirmed by Darwin
26 MARCH 2001, FLORIDA

Woman attempts to make a bigger ass of herself . . . and succeeds.

Many women wish to reduce the size of their posteriors, but a select few are more interested in enhancing it. One such woman, a fifty-three-year-old Fort Lauderdale resident, had exhausted a number of less invasive home remedies such as wearing padded layers of underwear, and moved on to surgical intervention.

She persuaded an unlicensed, underground "plastic surgeon" to boost her derriere by pumping it full of silicone in the comfort of her own living room. Shortly thereafter, hospital officials contacted police to report the suspicious death of the needle-marked woman, who had been delivered to the emergency room by rescue workers after suffering breathing difficulties in her apartment.

Reference: Reuters

DARWIN AWARD: THIRST FOR DEATH

Unconfirmed by Darwin
18 JANUARY 2001, NEW ZEALAND

She was dying for a cuppa.

The west coast of New Zealand is threaded with narrow, windy mountain roads that climb and descend the hills at improbable angles. A Christchurch driver with little patience for those dangerous curves was preparing a hot cup of tea in her car when she learned one last lesson about respect for the road.

Nothing, but nothing, could keep her from her afternoon tea that day. Well, all right, one thing could keep her from her tea. Karma. While she was trying to brew a cuppa, her car plunged over a precipice and into a creek. The woman was found dead three days later, still holding a box of tea bags, with a mug wedged against the steering wheel and a thermos of hot water beneath her feet.

There were no brake marks on the road.

Reference: *New Zealand Press*

Curious readers have questioned the veracity of this story, as some of the details seem implausible. Why was the water still hot? How could the accident kill the woman but not break the mug? And why didn't she lose her grip on the tea bags?
Join the debate!
www.DarwinAwards.com/book/tea.html

DARWIN AWARD: ANTS' REVENGE
Confirmed by Darwin
14 MAY 2001, NEW YORK

Proof that smoking is bad for your health.

A woman was found burned to death, her body still blazing on a grassy area adjacent to her home in Rome. A lighter and a melted gas can were discovered nearby. After a lengthy investigation police turned up no evidence of foul play. They believe her demise was due to her habit of dousing anthills with gasoline while she smoked cigarettes.

Reference: *Syracuse News*

Evolution Fights Back

HONORABLE MENTION: ROB PETER TO PAY PAUL

Confirmed by Darwin
16 JULY 2001, TENNESSEE

A woman ordered to make good on $1,100 in bad checks left the Union City courthouse, drove to her hometown, and pulled a gun on employees at the First State Bank. She fled into a cornfield with $7,000, eluded a hastily organized search party, and made her way back to Union City to pay her debt.

But given the small size of her town, with a population of 344, it was inevitable that one of the bank employees would recognize her. When she returned home, police were waiting to arrest her and confiscate the remainder of the money.

Reference: *Boston Globe*

Stupid Human Tricks

HONORABLE MENTION: CHILD PANDERING
Confirmed by Darwin
19 OCTOBER 2002, PORTUGAL

Parents, take note! Catering to a child's tantrum can have serious repercussions, as a Caldelas mother recently discovered. When her four-year-old son refused to eat his soup unless she let him play with a gun, she handed it over—and was promptly shot in the stomach by an accidental discharge. Although she survived, her dangerously questionable parenting practices earn her an Honorable Mention.

Reference: *Agence France-Presse*, news.com.au

Adding Insult to Injury

HONORABLE MENTION: HIPPO HOP

Confirmed by Darwin
31 JULY 2001, UKRAINE

A woman hopped the fence at Kharkiv Zoo in order to swim with Masha the Hippopotamus. But the woman's play time was cut short when the three-ton herbivore abruptly changed its dietary habit and mauled the intruder, in defense of her offspring.

Zoo officials said the woman's action was far from unusual. Visitors commonly ignore warning signs and fences, seeking to cavort with the animals.

The sinking swimmer was rescued from the irate mammal by irate zoo workers, who sent her to the hospital for treatment. Another free spirit learns a painful lesson while frolicking with large zoo animals!

Reference: Reuters, news.excite.com

Nature's UNDO key

The herbivorous hippo plays an important role in the African ecosystem. Hippo dung feeds tiny water microorganisms, which in turn support a food chain of larger creatures. On land the hippos' large bodies and grazing habits make trails that provide other animals with easy access to water holes.

African legend says the hippo was created to cut grass for the other animals. The hippo asked if she could stay in the water during the hot days, but God feared that she would eat all the fish. The hippopotamus promised to abstain, so God agreed. To this day she keeps her promise, dwelling in the water during the day and emerging to eat grass in the cool night air.

HONORABLE MENTION: OUT OF GAS
Confirmed by Darwin
20 JULY 2001, KANSAS

A woman who robbed two Wichita banks in one week, Bank of America and Emprise Bank, was captured when she forgot to attend to one small detail: filling her gas tank. After the second robbery she leapt into a waiting getaway car and sped off—but not before a witness memorized its license plate number and relayed the information to police.

Officers nabbed the woman minutes later and a mile away at a gas station, where she had stopped to fill the tank and buy a carton of cigarettes.

Captain Max Tenbrook explained that robbers who get away fast are less likely to get caught. "Our best shot at catching them [is] right after it happens." Aspiring thieves would do well to memorize a simple rhyme:

"Fill the tank before you rob the bank."

Reference: *Wichita Eagle*

PERSONAL ACCOUNT: BEPPLES
CALIFORNIA

I have an eccentric ex-boyfriend—doesn't everyone?—who was the mad-inventor type. He was always devising innovative schemes. He would come out of the bathroom with a revolutionary idea for a toilet-paper holder. He would detect "gold" jewelry in thrift stores that no one else had recognized. We would spend romantic weekends in the Patent Library.

One summer afternoon we were driving in the country when we noticed some strange round balls hanging from the trees. We stopped to pick a bunch. They were amazingly light, and when you cut them open, they looked a bit like Styrofoam. Wow! A cheap natural packing material and all for the taking! No petroleum reserves depleted! He named them "bepples" and I put our collection on the fireplace mantel.

Eventually my ex-boyfriend moved out and into his own place. As a playful housewarming surprise I put a few bepples in his medicine chest.

Several days later I came home from work and noticed a large swarm of sickly wasplike creatures flying around my apartment. It only took me a short time to realize that the bepples were really dormant wasp nests!

I quickly alerted my ex and threw out the bepples before any harm could come to me or my cat.

Reference: Ellen M. Shehadeh, Personal Account

PERSONAL ACCOUNT: CURE FOR LICE
AUGUST 2002, TEXAS

My cosmetology-school instructor was answering questions concerning the common problem of head lice, when she told us the story of a woman who had caught the little parasites while working at a day-care center.

After consulting with her mother and grandmother the woman decided to stop by the local gas station instead of the local drugstore. You see, an old wives' tale holds that soaking one's hair and scalp in gasoline will kill the bugs. To some extent it is true; however, lice are not the only creatures liable to suffer damage during this procedure.

After soaking her head in gasoline the woman was in the mood for a cigarette. So she carefully washed her hands, covered her hair with a towel, and stepped outside to light up (no pun intended). Shortly thereafter the day-care worker was no more, although it is safe to say that she had rid herself of head lice.

I do not know which is more disturbing: that this woman was so lacking in common sense as to douse her head in gasoline and light a cigarette, or that she was entrusted with several children's lives on a daily basis.

Reference: Kathryn P. Plaster, Personal Account

PERSONAL ACCOUNT: ELECTRIC ECCENTRIC
2002

It used to be, the dumbest thing I ever did was to come out of the kitchen with my hands dripping wet and reach down to plug in a lamp. I got quite a shock, but the lamp still works.

But now there's a new "Dumbest Thing I Ever Did" story.

I was cleaning the greasy range hood over my stove with a sponge and a bucket of soapy dishwater. There I was, scrubbing away, bent partially upside down, when my brother dropped by. He began giving me grief about the improper cleaning method I was using.

I myself was a mess of grime, and my brother sat clean and natty, not lifting a finger, so naturally I became irritated. "How else should I clean it?!"

It turns out that his real concern was the burned-out light-bulb, across which I was sloshing soapy water. The socket was empty, and live.

"Water and electricity don't mix," he said.

I told him, dripping (heh heh) with sarcasm, "Yeah, THAT would be a problem if I were stupid enough to take my wet finger and stick it in the open socket . . . " which were the last words I heard for five minutes.

I apparently stuck my finger right in the socket.

Reference: Kim Brooks Wei, Personal Account

PERSONAL ACCOUNT: HOME IMPROVEMENT
7 AUGUST 2000, WASHINGTON

As a longtime fan of the Darwin Awards it is with embarrassment and chagrin that I find myself compelled to submit this Personal Account. Obviously I did not succeed in the requisite removal of myself from the gene pool, but only due to a last-minute reflex, not to deliberate action on my part. In fact, in retrospect there was no intelligent action in this entire scenario.

Thankfully, as a postmenopausal woman who had no business being on a ladder at my rural, secluded home where I temporarily reside alone, the matter of future gene-pool viability has already been settled by a wise and foresighted Mother Nature.

During the second week of my vacation I decided to work on a home-improvement project designed to address complaints from a neighbor regarding my dog's roaming and kleptomania.

I would install an overhead dog run! But upon checking the products available at our local hardware stores, I found nothing quite long enough for the area I had in mind.

So I purchased 140 feet of plastic-covered quarter-inch wire, two eyehooks, wire clamps, a pulley, and two 8-inch turnbuckles. I attached one end of the line and a turnbuckle to a tree at the back of my property. I connected the other end of the line to an eyehook and turnbuckle on the back of my house, adjacent to a small deck and patio door.

Everything was going well. It looked like I had designed and installed a project that I could proudly display to my significant other when he returned from his annual work assignment in Alaska. As I admired my work, I noted that there was still a considerable sag in the line as it spanned the long distance from house to property line.

Then I remembered the turnbuckles.

I mounted the stepladder next to the deck, steadied myself against the back of the house, pulled the line as tight as I could by hand, and made sure that it was secured with the clamps and could not slip. Then I turned to face the rear property line, so that I could watch as I tightened the screws of the turnbuckle to take up the slack in the line. I reached up with my right hand, grasped the turnbuckle above and behind me, and gave it a healthy twist.

Unfortunately I twisted it in the wrong direction.

The screws of the turnbuckle came unscrewed, leaving me holding the taut line, which yanked me upward and to the right, directly over the deck at an altitude of twelve feet. Natural reflexes being what they are, I let go of the line and looked over my shoulder to see the deck coming up toward my head. I put one arm out and succeeded in deflecting a headfirst landing, but heard a terrible crunching sound as my right elbow stood in for my head. The rest of my body landed between the ladder and the deck, a space already occupied by the wall-mounted hose reel, which fought valiantly with my left hip and arm for territorial rights. The wall and my head were engaged in a similar dispute.

A five-hour sojourn to the local hospital ended with a diagnosis of one severely dislocated and broken elbow, one sprained wrist and thumb, a five-by-eight-inch goose egg already turning vivid shades of yellow and purple on my hip, more bruises covering my entire left forearm, and a nasty bump on the head.

As I write this, I am at the end of my second week in a splint, and I face many weeks of healing and physical therapy. I cannot work at my usual job as a correctional officer, and the dog is nowhere to be found—undoubtedly making his rounds of the neighborhood, stealing food, socks, and mittens from the local children.

Reference: Cyndi Julian, Personal Account

Give up! The stone wall always wins!

PERSONAL ACCOUNT: LION LUNCH
2002, SOUTH AFRICA

As a ranger I am inured to the stupidity of the public when confronted with wild animals, but my daughter's experience in Africa takes the cake. She worked in the Kruger National Park, where park authorities are scrupulous about warning people to remain within their cars at all times. A tourist driving through the park was motivated to ignore the rules when she spotted a lioness and her cubs. The woman's husband recalls her saying the cubs were not posed correctly, so she nipped out of the car and picked one up to move it closer to its siblings. Needless to say, the lioness shared her unexpected fresh lunch with the cubs.

Reference: Tom Hastings, Personal Account

Next!

CHAPTER 5

Technology:
Deus ex Machina

Though the mills of God grind slowly,
yet they grind exceeding small.
Though with patience He stands waiting,
with exactness grinds He all.

—Friedrich von Logau

Deus ex machina (Latin for "God from the machine") is a theatrical term referring to a contrivance of playwrights faced by an irreconcilable plot line, who opt to have a god swoop down and untangle the situation. The heroes in this chapter contrive to find themselves in perilous juxtaposition to their machinery, situations from which they require divine intervention to survive—or not!

BEWARE
FALLING
NUMERALS

DISCUSSION: ARGUMENTS FROM THE
DAWN OF LIFE

abiogenesis: n.
The development of living organisms from
nonliving matter, as opposed to biogenesis.
Also called autogenesis or spontaneous generation.

A ll life on Earth appears to share a common origin. Cells are filled with an aqueous solution containing an abundance of trace elements similar to seawater. Animals, plants, and viruses all make use of identical amino acids and nucleic acids—a small subset of the possible variations—and identical forms of DNA and RNA molecules. But how did life begin?

When planets of the solar system coalesced 4.6 billion years ago, the Earth was a hot and violent place. It was geothermally active and covered with seas sloshing in their basins under the pull of the moon. Because the atmosphere held no oxygen, there was no ozone layer to filter the photons, so the planet's surface was bombarded with ultraviolet radiation.

However, the air did contain significant amounts of carbon monoxide, methane, and ammonia, which are scant today. These simple molecules, CO, CH_4, and NH_3, can be combined in the laboratory to form complex organic molecules. In a famous 1953 experiment Harold Urey and Stanley Miller assembled a device that reproduced hypothetical early atmosphere mixtures. They eventually identified most of the amino acids that comprise proteins, as well as numerous sugars and lipids (fats).

The early Earth was definitely host to a brew of bioactive molecules in an environment rich in energy sources: heat, radiation, and tidal forces. But how that natural laboratory flask produced the first self-replicating molecules is not known. It's possible that they came into existence when smaller molecules aligned in close proximity on the surface of charged clays and rocky minerals, such as pyrite, and were chemically joined into macromolecules by the alternate wetting and drying of the tides. Or perhaps macromolecules were first created under high pressure near heat vents on the ocean floor.

These molecules appeared approximately 3.5 billion years ago, six hundred million years after the Earth's crust began to cool. We suspect that the earliest self-replicating macromolecules were RNA and small proteins, as they have catalytic properties and are found in all organisms. Unfortunately we have no examples of the earliest replicators, probably because the conditions necessary for their reproduction are no longer present. However, they were probably similar to today's retroviruses and prions: disease-causing RNA and protein molecules that are able to replicate themselves in a host organism.

The origin of cells, the next step above replicating macromolecules, is not as mysterious. Lipids, the major constituents of cell membranes, form spherical "micelles" when agitated in water. It's believed that the earliest cells self-assembled naturally, as self-replicating macromolecules embedded in lipid micelles. Some versions were, by chance, able to utilize interesting

features of the membrane such as its ability to separate a gradient across which energy could be generated. Once a self-replicating population of cells formed, more copies could be generated indefinitely, as long as offspring existed in a hospitable environment.

Conditions were apparently stable enough, or organisms became widespread quickly enough, that an unbroken continuum of life has existed on this planet since that time. Over billions of years the cell, the basis for all life, evolved into the complex variety of species we see around us and in the fossil record. We have available for study a continuous spectrum of living examples: from simple single-celled bacteria without a nucleus, to complex nucleated yeast cells, to multicellular sponge colonies of independent and unspecialized cells, to groups of specialized cells performing separate but mutually dependent functions, such as polar bears.

Are we sure that's what happened?

No, we're not. These are only educated guesses based on scientific knowledge. We have no examples of these hypothetical original life-forms, and not even the simplest self-replicating molecule has been created in the laboratory through random chemical interactions. It is theorized that millions of years of evolution led from simple organic molecules to self-replicating cells, but since the steps cannot be experimentally reproduced, we can only speculate about the origin of cells.

Chance certainly played a large role in the emergence of life on Earth. For instance, if we didn't have a massive moon to create tides, conditions might never have been hospitable for abiogenesis. Or if there had been less water, the small patches of life might not have been able to increase their range and would have been far more susceptible to destruction under extreme environmental conditions. Whether those primitive rep-licating life-forms would survive or die out may have been the most uncertain point in our evolution.

Less uncertain, of course, were the survival prospects of the Darwin winners on the following pages!

References:
Campbell, *Biology* (1987)
Goldsmith, *The Evolving Universe* (1985)
www.uwinnipeg.ca/~simmons/1116/16origin.htm
www.arn.org/docs/odesign/od171/rnaworld171.htm
web.mit.edu/newsoffice/tt/1998/oct28/bartel.html

We now know the atmosphere was less oxi-dizing and thus less likely to form the organic compounds distilled from the Miller-Urey appara-tus. Specific refutations of this and other dawn-of-life theories:

www.DarwinAwards.com/book/life.html

DARWIN AWARD: WHAT'S THAT SOUND?

Confirmed by Darwin

2 AUGUST 2002, KANSAS

Police said an Olathe man was struck and killed by a train after his vehicle broke down on Interstate 35. His attempts at repairing his car had failed, and he had stepped away from the busy freeway to call for help.

As luck would have it, he chose to stand on the train tracks paralleling the road. When the train engineer spotted him standing on the tracks, the man was holding a cell phone to one ear and cupping his hand to the other ear to block the noise of the oncoming locomotive.

Reference: *Kansas City Star*, KCTV Channel 5 News, eyewitnesses.

DARWIN AWARD: PIG JIG

Confirmed by Darwin

24 NOVEMBER 2001, HUNGARY

Two farmers were killed and a third was hospitalized with serious injuries after the men attempted to kill a pig with a home-made stun gun during a traditional Hungarian pre-Christmas slaughter.

One farmer electrocuted himself with the jury-rigged device during an unsuccessful attempt to knock out the pig. The elderly owner of the pig was so alarmed at the tragedy unfolding before his eyes that he suffered a heart attack and died.

The third farmer tried to come to the rescue of the first farmer by pulling the plug out of the socket. He was shocked, but survived.

Reference: Magyar Hírlap, Ananova.com

DARWIN AWARD: SLOW LEARNERS

Unconfirmed by Darwin
23 MARCH 2001, VIRGINIA

Derek, twenty-one, was driving to the courthouse to face charges of reckless unlicensed driving, speeding, and failure to wear seat belts, when he lost control of his speeding vehicle.

The Hyundai crossed the median of Interstate 64 and collided with a truck pulling a flatbed trailer carrying three cars. As luck would have it, Derek had again chosen not to wear his seat belt. He was ejected from the car and died at the scene.

MARCH 2001, NORTH CAROLINA

Caleb's tale is more complicated, but his fate is equally apt. Failure to wear his seat belt caused him to spend eighteen days in a coma, after he crashed his car at ninety miles per hour and was ejected from a window. But that was only his first mistake.

One year later Caleb was riding with a friend, again sans seat belt, when the speeding vehicle careened off the pavement. Once again he was involuntarily ejected from the window, only this time he was killed on impact.

Reference: *Norfolk Daily Press, Raleigh News & Observer*

Darwin Award: Stay with the Herd!

Confirmed by Darwin

20 June 1999, Seattle, Washington

Scenic cliffs abound on the slopes of Mount Rainier, and falling deaths are common on the 14,411-foot dormant volcano. But that didn't deter one snowboarder, who declined a ranger's invitation to join a group he was escorting safely down the mountain during inclement weather.

William left ten-thousand-foot Camp Muir and set out to conquer the unfamiliar terrain without cold-weather clothing or survival gear. The lone man disappeared into the heavy fog and drizzle, blundered over a waterfall, and landed at the edge of the Nisqually Glacier, four thousand feet below his starting point.

The body of the twenty-eight-year-old doctor was found beneath the waterfall two years later by park rangers searching for a group of recently missing climbers, who were rescued unhurt.

"We knew he was gone," William's father said. "It would have been wonderful if he [had] remained as part of the mountain."

Reference: Associated Press, *Albany (Oregon) Democrat-Herald*

Darwin Award: Coke Is It!

Confirmed by Darwin

12 December 1998, Canada

A man crushed beneath a vending machine while trying to shake loose a free soda? If you think it's an Urban Legend, you're wrong! Kevin, a nineteen-year-old Quebec student, killed himself at Bishop's University while shaking a 420-kilogram Coke machine. He had been celebrating the end of final exams with friends. He died beneath the soda machine, asphyxiated, with a blood alcohol level slightly over the legal driving limit.

Kevin's last act was committed in vain. "Even as it fell over, the vending machine did not let out a single can," the coroner reported.

Soda drinkers take note! The report also states that toppled vending machines have caused at least 35 deaths and 140 injuries in the last twenty years.

A spokesperson for Coke said that Canadian machines are now labeled with the warning, Tipping or Rocking May Cause Injury or Death. They have also installed antitheft devices in newer models to keep people from obtaining free drinks.

Reference: *The Canadian Press*, cokemachineaccidents.com,
National Post

Kevin's family questions the official report on his death and created a website to clear his name. Their explanation for why Kevin's death was not his fault? Shaking vending machines "was common practice at the university," and anyway, unknown persons might have crushed Kevin with the vending machine in a bizarre murder, as it "would be difficult for one person to move" the heavy machine.

Reader Comments:
"Coming soon: MAVEM, Mothers Against Vending Machines."
"It's safer to celebrate finals with beer."
"I guess Coke doesn't add life."

Read their version of the incident:
www.DarwinAwards.com/book/coke.html

DARWIN AWARD: WHERE'S THE CHUTE?

Confirmed by Darwin

NORTH CAROLINA, 1987

Ivan, an experienced parachutist with eight hundred jumps under his belt, was videotaping a private lesson given by an instructor for a single trainee. He had attached the video camera to his helmet so that it would capture the entire day of instruction, and the supporting power supply and recorder were in a heavy satchel slung on his back.

The group went up in the plane, and the instructor led the enthusiastic beginner through preparations for the jump. Ivan carefully documented the lesson, which needed to be perfect for the sake of posterity.

When they reached the jump site, Ivan jumped from the back of the plane and filmed the student and instructor jumping from the front of the plane. A few heartbeats later, tape still running, Ivan realized that he had been so focused on filming the jump that he had forgotten to strap on his own parachute. An FAA spokesperson said that he may have mistaken the weight of the video equipment strapped to his back for a parachute.

In the footage salvaged from the camera and spliced together, the student and instructor are shown in free fall before they pull their ripcords and recede rapidly from view. Then the cameraman's hands reach for his own ripcord. When Ivan realizes he has no ripcord, ergo no chute, his hands are seen to flail about wildly, then the camera pans down toward the approaching earth. . . .

Film from the final stage of the plunge was destroyed on impact.

Reference: Associated Press, *The Washington Post*,
UPI, *Charlotte Observer*

**You do not need a parachute to skydive.
You only need a parachute to skydive twice.**

DARWIN AWARD: JET TAXI

Confirmed by Darwin
30 JANUARY 2002, BRAZIL

Airport taxi drivers frequently hear the announcement "The white zone is for loading and unloading of passengers only." Now Santos Dumont Airport in Rio de Janeiro may need to add a new phrase: "The runway is for takeoff and landing of airplanes only."

"The signs that tell you to stop when the plane is on the runway are practically invisible," said the director of the local taxi cooperative. Apparently a Boeing 737 preparing for takeoff was equally invisible to one sixty-four-year-old taxi driver, who ignored a red light and sped across the runway after dropping off his fare. He was right behind the jet when it revved its engines in preparation for a 140-mile-per-hour takeoff.

Local aviation experts say the force of the 737's jets is comparable to that of a hurricane, but much hotter. The taxi spun seventy-five feet through the air, hit the rocks at Guanabara Bay, and ejected its driver, who wasn't wearing a seat belt.

The man's tip for the trip was a broken skull and thorax. He died in a coma four days later. Airport authorities cited driver error as the cause of the accident.

Reference: Reuters

A Rio de Janeiro reader confirms that the man died four days after the accident. The taxi was on a road that crosses just beyond the airport runway, and he should have stopped at the red light that indicates an airplane is taking off or landing. The Civilian Aviation Department, a federal agency, published a report concluding that the traffic light was working perfectly and that the accident was caused by the taxi driver's "imprudent action."

DARWIN AWARD: MECHANIC MAYHEM
Confirmed by Darwin
15 JANUARY 2002, WASHINGTON

A forty-nine-year-old Boeing worker was performing maintenance on a giant, computer-controlled machine that makes parts
out of metal blocks, using hydraulics to control its movement.
The hydraulic lines are pressurized to twenty thousand pounds
per square inch even when the machine is shut off. Working on
equipment such as this requires attention to detail, and a careless
employee is liable to suffer dire consequences.

The potential for trouble should have been obvious to this
sixteen-year member of the Machinists Union, and yet, despite
redundant safety procedures, tags, warning signs, and a fearful
coworker, our Darwin Award hopeful began to remove a hydraulic line without relieving the pressure.

The bolts holding the line in place were so tight that he had
to locate a four-foot section of pipe to attach to his ratchet to
give him enough leverage to loosen the bolt. For some that
would have been warning enough that the line was pressurized.

Four high-strength bolts attached the line to the machine. The
soon-to-be-ex-employee had removed three, and loosened the
fourth, when the overstressed bolt snapped. A foot-long, three-
inch-diameter brass sleeve was inside the line to prevent the
hose from kinking. It shot out and hit the mechanic in the fore-
head with such force that it knocked him back eight feet, ricocheted off his head, and struck a crane fifty feet overhead.

The maintenance worker never knew what hit him.

Reference: Eyewitness accounts, Boeing news release.

The details of this event come from eyewitness reports and a news release from Boeing. The precise details are disputed, but the story is written to take as many observations into account as possible. To add facts, or read the most recent comments, visit the website:

www.DarwinAwards.com/book/boeing.html

Reader Comments:
"Tell Bob there may be a job opening in Auburn."
"Talk about a slap upside the head."
"Boeing . . . Boeing . . . Bong."

DARWIN AWARD: PATH OF LEAST RESISTANCE

Unconfirmed by Darwin

2001, CALIFORNIA

A man whose parked car began to roll into a reservoir near Fresno leapt in front of it and tried to physically prevent it from seeking lower ground. But this was not a case of an irresistible force (the car) meeting an immovable object (the man). Instead of stopping, the vehicle rolled over its owner, pinning him beneath the water and drowning him.

Darwin and Newton share a hearty laugh.

DARWIN AWARD: PRECARIOUS PERCH

Confirmed by Darwin

2 OCTOBER 2001, KANSAS

Brent, a thirty-one-year-old bow hunter, defied tradition by getting himself killed not with a stray arrow, but with electricity. The accomplished bowman had placed his hunting stand on what he thought was an abandoned utility pole, but when he touched the two live wires, he discovered the error of his ways.

Brent's body was discovered four days later. His two faithful Labrador retrievers were found waiting near his truck.

Friends were surprised by the accident. "Brent was always such a cautious and safe guy. Whatever took place that day, I'm sure he studied it and somehow came to the conclusion that those lines had to be dead."

It was a mistake that cost him his life.

29 SEPTEMBER 2001, PENNSYLVANIA

In a similar mishap another bow hunter set up a hunting blind on a utility pole in the trees. When he climbed onto the perch, he touched two electrified wires and was knocked to the ground by the power surge. This lucky hunter survived.

Reference: *Pittsburgh Post-Gazette,* TheDenverChannel.com,
Associated Press, *Wichita Eagle*

Power poles are private property, and
climbing them is considered trespassing.

Natural Selection in Action

DARWIN AWARD: SNEAKERS

Unconfirmed by Darwin

8 FEBRUARY 2002, PENNSYLVANIA

If the shoe fits . . .

Outside a camp for troubled youths, pairs of sneakers dangled from the electricity line, presumably tossed there by "troubled youths" who enjoyed the challenge and notoriety. But the sneakers were an eyesore to one twenty-year-old employee. They must be eliminated!

He stood in the raised bucket of a front-end loader and poked at the sneakers with a device consisting of a fourteen-foot copper tube with a metal pocketknife taped to the end. Copper is one of the most conductive substances known to man. The determined employee had nearly removed one pair of shoes, when the knife pierced the insulation and made contact with the electrical wire.

He was knocked out of the bucket and landed on the hood of the loader with burns on his hands, a foot, and his buttocks. He died from his injuries three weeks later.

Does his death seem the obvious result of a foolish choice? Not according to his mother, who said, "Nobody knows what really happened."

Reference: *The Derrick and News Herald*

DARWIN AWARD: THINK BEFORE YOU LEAP

Confirmed by Darwin
21 JULY 2001, IDAHO

When his brakes failed while driving down a steep mountain road, Marco bailed out on his eight passengers and leapt from his Dodge van. Too bad he didn't alert the others to the problem instead of taking flight so precipitously. Another passenger was able to bring the vehicle to a stop a short distance away. Marco struck his head on the pavement and died at the scene. No one else was injured.

Reference: *South Idaho Press*

Remember the old adage, He Who Hesitates is Lost? Not this time: He who hesitated, lived. Drivers have a responsibility to the occupants of their vehicle, and when Marco bailed out on that responsibility, he was rewarded by a karmic fate. Drivers should always try the emergency brake before leaping from a moving vehicle. The life you save could be your own!

DARWIN AWARD: THE WORM HAS TURNED

Unconfirmed by Darwin
OCTOBER 2002, NORWAY

It's a well-known fishing trick: put 12-volt electrodes into the ground, and worms will crawl to the surface. A car battery gets the job done. But a twenty-three-year-old Laagendalsposten man withdrew his genes from the pool when he tried to speed up the time-tested process. He figured that a 220-volt, 50-hertz line would bring more worms out faster, and he was prepared to put his theory to the test.

Alas, he did so while squatting on a steel bucket, holding an electrode in one hand with the other planted in the ground a few feet away. He seemed determined to enter the eternal fishing grounds. Quicker than spit, that wish was granted. Our Darwin winner leaves only parents—and no offspring—back by the earthly creek.

> **Alarmingly for those of us who know better than to stick live wires into the ground, this death is not an isolated incident. According to the U.S. Consumer Product Safety Commission, by 1993, electric "worm-getter" devices connected to 120-volt household current had caused the deaths of at least thirty people!**

Darwin Award: Bees 1, Humans 0

Unconfirmed by Darwin

23 September 2002, Brazil

A farm keeper from São Paulo decided to remove a beehive from his orange tree. He didn't know exactly how to proceed, but he knew the hive should be burned, and he knew bees sting. So he protected his head with a plastic bag sealed tightly around his neck, grabbed a torch, and went off to fight the bees.

His worried wife went to look for him a few hours later and found him dead. However, it wasn't the bees that killed him. The plastic bag had protected him from smoke, stingers, and . . . oxygen! He had forgotten to put breathing holes in the bag.

Reference: Folha Online

You are the weakest link. Good-bye!

DARWIN AWARD: TIED OFF

Unconfirmed by Darwin

IOWA

Give someone enough rope . . .

The Boone & Scenic Valley Railroad operated until the fifties, and is currently run as a tourist attraction. Its route includes the Kate Shelley Bridge, the highest and longest double-track railroad bridge in the world, rising 184 feet over the Des Moines River. The open train ride across the abyss is both stunningly beautiful and somewhat nerve-racking.

Several years ago an adventurous pair decided to take their ropes and rappel off this architectural support. Words can hardly describe how breathtakingly high the narrow bridge is. Our adventurers had to be completely fearless as they walked to the middle, tied off their ropes, and began to rappel down.

But when the Boone & Scenic Valley Railroad train came by on its daily tour of the valley, their one mistake became apparent. They had tied the ropes to the sturdiest support possible: the steel train tracks. . . .

Thus far the story is unconfirmed, but several versions have surfaced. The adventurers may have been Boy Scouts who tossed one rope across the tracks and rappelled down opposite sides. They may have been students from Iowa State University. Local residents remember similar stories that could be the basis of this account, and were told to children to keep them away from the bridge. One reader recalls a court case where the family of the deceased sued the railroad for not posting pedestrian warning signs.

Eyewitness and media reports are welcome!
www.DarwinAwards.com/book/railroad.html

Darwin Award: The Unkindest Cut

Confirmed by Darwin
30 May 2001, Oregon

"Improper use of pruning shears can dull the blades."

Ishmael, twenty-five, was driving a Toyota truck when he lost control of the vehicle, which careened into a mailbox, collided with a utility pole, and flipped onto its side, knocking down high-voltage power lines in the process. At that point Ishmael climbed from the truck and into the path of evolution.

He surveyed the situation with a pair of pruning shears in his hand. Police speculate that he reached up to clip the snaking, arcing cable lying across his truck and was electrocuted when the shears touched the 7,500-volt cable. A medical examination found that the current had traveled across his heart and out his left foot. He was found lying motionless, facedown on the power line, with a pair of pruning shears in his hands.

His dazed passenger survived to be arrested on an unrelated warrant.

Reference: *Portland Oregonian*

DARWIN AWARD: TRAIN OF THOUGHT

Unconfirmed by Darwin

SEPTEMBER 1989, RUSSIA

Illustrating the power of positive thinking.

The Soviet Union is home to a growing number of psychics and mentalists. One of them, L. Mandel, became convinced that he could use his powers to stop vehicles in their tracks.

Mandel started small—a bicycle here, an automobile there—before graduating to streetcars. Finally, he devised an ultimate test of his psychic power: He would halt a freight train in its tracks. He believed that "in extraordinary conditions of a direct threat to my organism, all my reserves will be called into action."

The engineer of the train that ran Mandel over saw him toss his briefcase aside and step onto the tracks with arms raised, head lowered, and body tensed. The engineer applied the emergency brakes, but it was too late.

The mentalist psyched himself out.

Reference: Associated Press

One wonders how many of the bicycles and cars Mandel "stopped" were just alert drivers able to hit the brakes before they turned him into road-kill. A person of average intellect, knowing that laws of physics dictate how long it takes a massive object to come to a complete stop, would presumably jump to safety at the last moment as he realized the "mind trick" wasn't working.

DARWIN AWARD: WIPED OUT

Unconfirmed by Darwin

4 SEPTEMBER 1999, TOKYO, JAPAN

"It's still not clean!"

Enishi was a part-time janitor until his eagerness to do a good job collided with an unhealthy inattention to his own safety. The elevator he was cleaning had water leaking from its ceiling, so he rode a second elevator up the shaft, climbed out its hidden side door, and hopped on top of the first elevator. As he cleaned the puddle from the roof, the car rose to the top floor, fatally crushing him beneath the ceiling of the building. The twenty-four-year-old had forgotten to turn off the leaking elevator before wiping up the spill, leaving the roof messier than before.

Reference: *Mainichi Daily News*

Several elevator facts argue against the veracity of this story. When a trapdoor is opened, a safety circuit is tripped, preventing the elevator from moving. Most elevators have two to six feet of clearance at the top of the shaft, and thus will not squash a person. And elevators have a "stop" button on the roof, so a person in the unenviable position of riding an elevator hurtling toward the sky has one last recourse.

Darwin Award: Wounded Wire Bites Back

Confirmed by Darwin

14 February 2002, Pennsylvania

Daniel and his friend were practicing their marksmanship by shooting at targets in a farm field. But instead of the usual choices of mice, bottles, or birds, they selected a more worthy adversary: electrical insulators.

These pear-shaped glass or plastic devices are intended to hold electrical wires aloft, but after the men shot six insulators off two utility poles, the shattered targets were no longer up to the job. A high-voltage wire fell to the ground and Daniel, attempting to prevent a fire, seized the sizzling wire in his hand and was electrocuted.

An Allegheny Power spokesperson advised people not to shoot at electrical insulators.

Reference: Hagerstown *Herald Mail*

DARWIN AWARD: ROMANIAN TRAINS

Confirmed by Darwin
JULY 2002, ROMANIA

Perhaps just looking down the track would have sufficed . . .

Forget posted train schedules! Like an American Indian listening for horses in an old Western, a Romanian man placed his ear against the tracks to listen for the arrival of a train scheduled to stop at his station. The forty-six-year-old man was hit by an express train and died instantly from head trauma.

Apparently it's true, you don't hear the bullet that hit you!

Reference: Ananova.com

Tragic Proof of a Missing "Why?" Chromosome

DARWIN AWARD: HIGH ON GRASS

Confirmed by Darwin
30 SEPTEMBER 2000, NEW MEXICO

A father-and-son team hired to mow the grass at the Tucumcari Municipal Airport decided that their skills with the lawn mower would suffice for a joyride in an airplane. Although neither was a certified pilot, or indeed even a student pilot, they managed to taxi the private two-seater to the fueling facility, fill the tanks, and taxi to the runway, where they commenced a takeoff.

That's when their luck ran out. A hundred fifty feet above the airport the plane began to wobble, then entered a vertical dive and collided with the grass. The men managed to escape from the mangled aircraft before a post-impact fire destroyed it. The men are living examples that training and a license may not be needed to mow the lawn but are necessary requirements for flying a plane.

Reference: www.ntsb.gov ID#DEN00FA183

HONORABLE MENTION:
(UN)ARMED AND DANGEROUS
Confirmed by Darwin
NOVEMBER 2001, SOUTH WALES

A drunk driver? No Darwin.

A one-armed man driving an unadapted car? No Darwin.

A man driving while talking on a cell phone? No Darwin.

But a drunken one-armed man driving an unadapted car while talking on a cell phone? Darwin Award—almost! Charles was stopped by police after driving through a red traffic light while holding a mobile phone to his ear with his good arm. His other arm, missing below the elbow, was no help with the gears and steering.

Charles had almost twice the legal limit of alcohol on his breath. He nearly forfeited his life but instead forfeited his license. The rest of us were granted an eighteen-month reprieve from his presence behind the wheel, and Charles wins only an Honorable Mention as one of the lucky few who manage to evade a seemingly certain doom.

One wonders where his missing arm went!

Reference: BBC News, Ananova.com

HONORABLE MENTION: DUCT TAPE TEACHER

Confirmed by Darwin

SEPTEMBER 2001, OHIO

A forty-nine-year-old physics teacher allowed students to duct-tape him to a wall as part of a high school fund-raising event. But duct tape, unlike ordinary garments, doesn't "breathe." Eighty minutes and ninety-two pieces of duct tape into the process, the teacher overheated and lost consciousness. He confided later, "I had some fantastic dreams while I was out." Doctors said the stunt would have been fatal, if students hadn't acted quickly and released him from his silver bonds.

Reference: *Akron Beacon Journal*, whirlygirl.com

**See photos of people duct taped to walls:
www.DarwinAwards.com/book/ducttape.html**

HONORABLE MENTION: STINGY SCIENTIST
1966, AUSTRALIA

Against animal testing? How about human animal testing?

Dr. Jack Barnes, of Cairns, Australia, failed to halt the spread of his own mad-scientist genes, but his survival wasn't due to a lack of effort on his part. In 1966 Barnes was hot on the heels of a mysterious illness called Irukandji syndrome. Sufferers endure excruciating back pain, sweating, and nausea. He suspected that the source of the illness was a tiny marine creature, so he set about finding it by sitting on the seabed for hours, wearing a weighted diving suit. Note the outstanding Darwin potential already demonstrated.

However, the Grim Reaper did not yet beckon. Instead, the fickle finger of fate rewarded him by revealing the source of the mystery illness: a minute jellyfish, its bell measuring only an inch across. It was at this point that the doctor's latent Darwin potential, already hinted at, was unleashed to its full (and nearly fatal) potential.

There are many toxic jellyfish off the coast of Australia. Our dedicated scientist knew he must test his hypothesis that this gelatinous creature was toting the particular venom that causes Irukandji syndrome. And how best to go about this?

He chose the most expedient method available: He stung himself.

Foolish? Yes, but the good doctor was not done yet. To reach truly dizzying heights of Darwinian grandeur one must ensure that one's deficient DNA is entirely removed from the gene pool. As Dr. Barnes had already sired an heir, there was only one thing left to do. . . .

He stung his fourteen-year-old son as well!

Despite this truly outstanding effort to place the continued existence of the Barnes lineage in mortal peril—alas, it wasn't to be. Dr. Barnes, his son, and the nearby lifeguard whom the good doctor also introduced to the joys of Irukandji syndrome were all rushed to the intensive care unit of a nearby hospital. All three survived.

As a final twist, not only will the mad scientist's genes live on, but so, too, will the family name: The jellyfish was named *Carukia barnesi* in honor of the intrepid scientist!

Reference: Reuters

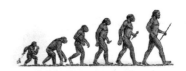

HONORABLE MENTION: SHED PROTECTION
Unconfirmed by Darwin
AUGUST 2002, THE NETHERLANDS

A sixty-six-year-old Margraten resident wanted to protect his garden shed against burglars. The best way to do this, he decided, was to construct a booby trap. He cobbled together some ropes and a shotgun aimed at the door. Proud of his ingenuity, he demonstrated the effectiveness of the device to two friends by shooting himself in the abdomen and lower arm. An emergency operation prevented him from winning a Darwin Award. Police searched his home and confiscated firearms and ammo, along with fifteen full-grown marijuana plants that perhaps had helped him formulate this painful lesson in safety.

Reference: *Dagblad De Limburger*, www.limburger.nl

Evolution's Revenge

HONORABLE MENTION: WILD SHOT

Confirmed by Darwin
26 MARCH 2002, MONTANA

Another gem from the FAA accident reports! A pilot and his passenger were hunting coyotes from the air, when the passenger accidentally discharged his shotgun into the right wing of the aircraft, causing the plane to crash. The two hunters were injured but survived, as did the fortunate coyotes.

Reference: FAA accident reports

**In the ongoing battle between airplanes
and the ground, the ground has yet to lose.**

HONORABLE MENTION: NAILED!

Confirmed by Darwin

23 JANUARY 2001, PENNSYLVANIA

Every home needs a handyman for those essential remodeling tasks. But not every homeowner knows how to get the job done, so professionals are sometimes called in to help. Enter Malcolm, twenty-five, whose employer sent him to the home of a Bethlehem man to help renovate the basement.

Malcolm was using a portable miter saw that requires quite a bit of concentration. When our hero's attention slipped, so did the saw, which sliced off his hand at the wrist. As if losing a limb weren't bad enough, the injured man proceeded to shoot himself in the head a dozen times with a pneumatic nail gun in an attempt to end his misery.

The homeowner ventured downstairs to check on the remodeling, but to his surprise the basement seemed to be empty. He was about to leave when his dog discovered Malcolm whimpering in the corner, nails protruding from his scalp.

The owner of the company arrived at the scene, located the missing limb, wrapped it in a clean plastic sandwich bag, and sent it with Malcolm to the hospital. A dozen one-and-a-half-inch nails were removed from Malcolm's head at St. Luke's Hospital in Fountain Hill, and the severed hand was reattached.

Reference: *Bethlehem Morning Call*, CNN.com, The Associated Press

**More proof that nail guns
and skulls don't mix.
1 January 2000, Ohio**

Stanley was playing around with a nail gun when he shot himself in the head at a New Year's Eve party. But he didn't get medical treatment until the next day when his boss noticed a nasty bruise on his head and sent him to the hospital. A one-and-a-half-inch nail was removed from his skull, slightly increasing the airspace already present.

Reference: The Associated Press.

PERSONAL ACCOUNT: XYZ
PACIFIC OCEAN

Every other year sailors board sailboats in San Francisco, and spend eleven or twelve days racing to Hawaii, pushing hard day and night. Crew members never sleep more than three hours at a stretch. Sooner or later they need to bathe. Unfortunately, racing sailboats save weight by carrying the minimum required amount of freshwater, and few have pressurized hot water. So the bathing routine consists of stripping down on deck, throwing a bucket over the side to scoop up some seawater, and scrubbing up.

A persistent marine layer of clouds typically occludes the sun for the first three days out of San Francisco. Even if the sun appears a few days out, the air temperature is still in the low sixties and the water temperature is even lower. These conditions are not terribly inviting to bathers. So sometime around day seven, one finally breaks down (or the rest of the crew insists) and decides to bathe.

Given that the bather plans to soap up, and things will be slippery, the standard procedure is to don a harness attached to the boat with a tether. And since the boat is generally moving fast enough to rip a bucket right out of your hand—and the next stop to pick up a new bucket is a week in the future—it's also important to tether the bucket.

In a recent Pacific Cup race a crew member allegedly put on his harness, and while he didn't tether himself to the boat, he very carefully tied the bucket to his harness before throwing it overboard.

The boat went back to pick him up. Some might argue that this was an error in judgment, but it happens to be required by the rules!

On a related matter . . .

Every year a number of people fall off a boat at sea and die. Most of them happen to be men, and reports claim that the majority are found with their flies open. The theory is that they took a leak over the rail before going off watch, ignoring safety precautions like clipping on, and fell or were washed overboard.

Now, this seems puzzling. Suppose you found yourself suddenly washed overboard in the middle of the ocean. Unless you banged into something on the way down, you wouldn't die instantly. If it were you, knowing you'd be swimming for some time before you drowned, wouldn't you take a moment to tuck things back in place and zip up, lest the fishies start nibbling? Or are they trying to survive longer by using their tackle as bait?

These statistics are rumored to come from the Coast Guard, yet they smack of Urban Legend status. Either way it seems like there's potentially interesting fodder for the Darwin Awards here.

Reference: Anonymous Personal Account

PERSONAL ACCOUNT: LASER DIM BULB
2002

Of the numerous items found in machine shops that can be hazardous to your health, industrial lasers are among the scariest.

These lasers can burn a hole through inch-thick steel in seconds. Unlike a sharp blade, or the flame of a welding torch, a laser beam can extend hundreds of feet with its power undiminished. And to add more raw danger, these laser beams are usually completely invisible, unlike the depictions one sees in movies. Serious precautions surround the use of industrial lasers. For instance, their mountings make it impossible to point them at a human.

Despite such safety devices, *some* people positively *should not* be allowed to work with lasers!

Service technicians were installing a new type of laser in a factory, and testing the accuracy of its aim by firing it at a plastic block. The laser burns a hole through the block, and by assessing the shape of the hole, one determines how tightly the beam is focused. This test is usually performed with a horizontal laser beam emitted by a laser clamped horizontally across a block. But the technicians had no blocks at hand, so they asked a factory machinist to hold up the block, while the technicians fired the unclamped, and wobbly, laser.

What were they thinking?

The beam missed the block entirely and hit the machinist's hand, causing severe burns. It was lucky for him that the beam was not yet focused. He was whisked away to the emergency room, and returned to work with his left arm swathed in bandages.

Reference: A person who works in the machine tool industry, Personal Account

PERSONAL ACCOUNT: BICYCLE BLUES
2000

When my friend and I were kids, I rode a ten-speed and he had a funky little bike whose pedals moved in tandem with the front tire. I dared him to ride down a steep slope of road on his bike. With no more than mild encouragement, down he went. I cheered him on as I rode down with him on my trusty ten-speed in case he ran into trouble.

The faster he went, the faster those pedals whizzed around. As he neared the foot of the hill, he began to panic because he couldn't hit the handbrakes (there weren't any) and he couldn't apply the pedal brakes because the pedals were spinning too fast. I yelled to him to slow the front tire with his shoes.

So what did he do?

He stuck his feet into the spokes of the tire. You can imagine the chain reaction as his feet halted the movement of the tire, causing the bike to flip and buck the lad off the seat. He did a few air somersaults, landed on his head, and slid along ten feet of asphalt, with the bike flipping to land several feet in front of him.

He walked out of the hospital with road rash and a few stitches behind his ear, and swore off that evil bike . . . for a few weeks, anyway.

Reference: Anonymous Personal Account

PERSONAL ACCOUNT: STALLED MOTORCYCLE
SEPTEMBER 2001, VIRGINIA

Those who work in motorcycle shops see many who have no business being atop two wheels. One particular man who brought his bike in for service was a classic example. The entire front end of his bike had been ripped clean off—an odd damage pattern. By way of explanation he offered the following tale.

The motorcycle had sat idle for several months. When he eventually tried to start it again, time had drained the battery. Fortunately, he knew that a manual-transmission vehicle, rolling with sufficient speed and popped into second gear, will often start right up. So he attempted to bump-start it.

The owner lived at the top of a long hill. After repeated and unsuccessful attempts to bump-start the bike on the way down, he was left with a new problem: a stalled bike sitting at the bottom of a long incline.

The man called his girlfriend and asked her to bring her truck so he could tow the bike back up the hill. A length of rope was procured, and one end of the rope was affixed to the truck's bumper. The other end was affixed to the waist of the bike owner, who planned to ride the stalled motorcycle up the hill.

They set off, she in her truck and he on his bike, and all was well until he decided to make one final bump-start attempt. As soon as the clutch engaged, the engine turned into a brake. The bike stopped cold.

The owner did not.

His girlfriend was blissfully unaware of what was happening and proceeded to drive to his house, dragging his body slowly behind her. Despite his injuries and lack of sense he recovered to share his cautionary tale with the employees of his local motorcycle shop.

Reference: Anonymous Personal Account

**You can lead a man to knowledge,
but you can't make him think!**

PERSONAL ACCOUNT: ELECTRIC SAFETY LESSON
1990

All personnel stationed on an aircraft carrier are given safety lectures and demonstrations. In 1990 a first class petty officer assigned to the mess deck was briefing new junior personnel on electrical safety. He showed them how to fill out a warning tag on circuits undergoing maintenance, and informed them that they were forbidden to work on the circuit until a second person had double-checked the tag and circuit. In a prime demonstration of why the rules were in place, he proceeded to open and grab a circuit that he supposed was deenergized, killing himself in front of twenty thunderstruck students.

Reference: Anonymous Personal Account

Unnatural Selection

CHAPTER 6

Glory Days Gone

Not all submissions become Darwin Awards, and those that do are sometimes disqualified when new information comes to light, or extenuating circumstances are pointed out by readers. This chapter shows some of the stories that were nominated but ultimately disqualified for violating one or more "Darwinian" rules.

DISQUALIFIED DARWIN AWARD: HUMAN CATAPULT

Confirmed by Darwin

27 NOVEMBER 2002, ENGLAND

We have all seen films where a sieging army flattens the enemy's defenses by catapulting boulders through the air. Have you ever wondered what it feels like to be the boulder? Some people do, notably members of two Oxford student groups: the Human Catapult Club and the Oxford Stunt Factory.

A nineteen-year-old club member, climbed into a replica of a fifty-foot medieval trebuchet and catapulted himself toward a net some distance away. But—you guessed it—the human boulder missed that all-important safety device and fell to his death just short of the net.

The organizer of the catapult event said, "We calculated his weight and the power of the catapult. I don't know what went wrong." Unfortunate accident? Maybe, if not for the fact that inaccurate calculations had already sent one catapultee bouncing off the net to land headfirst on the ground. And in previous years the organizer's own girlfriend had suffered broken bones following her turn in the bucket.

A person who entrusts his life to a contraption powered by inaccurate projectile mathematics—a contraption that has already injured two people rather severely—is clearly a candidate for a Darwin Award.

Reference: ITV Evening News, *Oxford Student News*

Trebuchets were first powered by muscle, then by a massive counterweight that, when dropped, swung the long arm holding the load. During peacetime trebuchets were used to launch roses at ladies during tournaments. During war trebuchets were loaded with stone missiles to damage castle walls, with dung or animal corpses to spread disease, or with the severed heads of enemy soldiers to terrorize opponents.

Darwinian Rule Violation: Accident, not self-inflicted.

At first blush it seems phenomenally stupid to rocket oneself from a catapult. But a closer scrutiny of the facts, prompted by a complaint from a close friend, shows that the young man was actually the victim of an unfortunate tragedy.

Did the catapult operators say it was safe? Yes. Were there signs warning that being fired from the catapult could be deadly? No. Was there a safety net? Yes, the size of a tennis court. Was the deceased the only one to be fired from the trebuchet? No, five previous catapultees landed safely. Furthermore, two event organizers were later arrested and charged with manslaughter, indicating that authorities believe the deceased was not to blame.

If he had built the catapult himself and performed a test run using a few mattresses as his landing pad, then he would be eligible for a Darwin Award. But he had reason to believe he was taking part in a safe, albeit adventurous, stunt. Therefore, no Darwin!

DISQUALIFIED DARWIN AWARD:
BOOMERANG EFFECT

Confirmed by Darwin
FALL 2000, VIRGINIA

A man found himself paralyzed—and hence unable to reproduce—when he made the fatal decision to swerve and hit a dog with his truck. He missed the dog, and the vehicle careened out of control on the gravel road and tipped over an embankment. His son and a passenger were rescued, unhurt. No one was wearing a seat belt. Police found a cooler of beer in the back and empty cans in the cab of the overturned vehicle. An officer stated, "They were out joy riding, bought lottery tickets, and just cut through that gravel road." As it turned out, the wrong lottery paid off.

Reference: *Lynchburg News & Advance*

Darwinian Rule Violation:
No astounding misapplication of judgment.

This story describes a case of poetic justice, but the action of swerving to hit a dog is simply not an outstandingly stupid decision, even though it shows an unappealing lack of empathy for animals. Most people who swerve to hit dogs survive. Although the story is disqualified on the grounds that it lacks excellence, the perpetrator is certainly a candidate for an instant karma award.

DISQUALIFIED DARWIN AWARD: COP CAP

Confirmed by Darwin

8 AUGUST 2001, MISSOURI

When the chief of police reached into the trunk of his patrol car and pulled out his shotgun, he should have remembered to point the gun aside. But even the best-trained men make mistakes. His "quick draw" precipitated a fatal self-shooting when the trigger caught on a loop of fabric, and he accidentally peppered himself with buckshot.

According to the sheriff, "The safety had been bumped into the firing position as the gun bounced around within the trunk," and the weapon was found to have "an unusually light trigger pull."

Reference: *Joplin Globe*, *Detroit News*, Associated Press

Darwinian Rule Violation:
No astounding misapplication of judgment.

This death was caused by an error in judgment, to be sure. Common safety procedures require a gun to be stored unloaded and, when handled, to be kept pointing in a safe direction, whether or not it is loaded. The chief of police was clearly acting unsafely, but nevertheless, he did not display an *astounding* lapse of judgment when he removed the weapon from the car. It was common carelessness, so no Darwin.

DISQUALIFIED DARWIN AWARD: NEXT TIME TRY A TAXI

Confirmed by Darwin

11 AUGUST 1999, TEXAS

A thirty-one-year-old Houston man spotted a truck left running as its driver filled jugs with filtered water from a vending machine. The idiot hopped into the truck, not realizing that four children were still occupying their seats. The mother heard a scream and turned to see her truck speeding away.

Normally a stolen car is not the target of urgent police attention, but in this case authorities could not stand by while children were in danger. A two-hour car chase on the freeways of Houston ensued. The chase came to a dramatic conclusion as the truck sped onto the Jesse Jones Toll Bridge, which stands 150 feet over the Houston shipping channel at its apex.

With police in hot pursuit, the truck accelerated from seventy-five to ninety mph, and the driver stuck his head out the window as he steered toward the right-side rail. He shifted into neutral and tried to jump from the window over the guardrail and into the seawater below. But in his haste he failed to notice the chain-link fence installed to thwart jumpers.

As the truck sideswiped the guardrail, the fence slammed into the car thief's skull, ripping "what was left of him" out the window. Adding insult to injury, his corpse was crushed by a large truck that had been following close behind.

The young occupants of the car suffered only minor scrapes and bruises.

Reference: *Houston Chronicle*, Harris County Deputies' Organization: The Voice of Law Enforcement

Darwinian Rule Violation:
No astounding misapplication of judgment.
Innocent bystanders injured.

This man put children in harm's way and almost certainly trau-matized them, so innocent bystanders were injured. Further-more, his manner of death—leaping from a car during a police chase—was not extraordinarily stupid, it was merely lurid. There-fore, the story violates two rules and is disqualified.

DISQUALIFIED DARWIN AWARD:
FATAL CUE

Confirmed by Darwin
15 FEBRUARY 2002, RUSSIA

A twenty-six-year-old man tried to enter a bar in Tomilino, near Moscow, carrying a concealed TT handgun. He was stopped by an alert security guard, whereupon the man menaced the guard with the weapon. The guard kicked it out of his hands, and the gun fell onto a billiards table.

The security guard asked the players to pass the gun over to him. One of them, our Darwin Award nominee, thought the best way to accomplish this task was to pick it up with his pool cue. The gun slid down the cue stick, and its increasing thickness was sufficient to push the trigger and shoot the nineteen-year-old in the chest. He died immediately.

The owner of the gun said he had intended to surrender the gun to the police that day, and went to the bar in order to summon courage from alcoholic libations. Since handguns are illegal in Russia, intent to surrender is a common, but improbable, claim. Handgun owners are even known to carry weapon-surrender letters in their wallets in case of arrest.

Reference: *Vecherniaya Moskva*, www.pyat.ru

Darwinian Rule Violation:
Accident, not self-inflicted.

This story has been disqualified because it's not obvious that one can kill oneself with a gun sliding down a stick. Because guns are outlawed in Russia, it's likely that the billiards player was unfamiliar with them. Picking up an unfamiliar weapon with a cue stick instead of one's hand is not outstandingly stupid behavior, and can arguably be considered a prudent act, so no Darwin for the deceased.

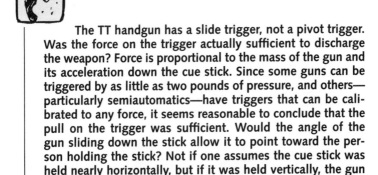

The TT handgun has a slide trigger, not a pivot trigger. Was the force on the trigger actually sufficient to discharge the weapon? Force is proportional to the mass of the gun and its acceleration down the cue stick. Since some guns can be triggered by as little as two pounds of pressure, and others—particularly semiautomatics—have triggers that can be calibrated to any force, it seems reasonable to conclude that the pull on the trigger was sufficient. Would the angle of the gun sliding down the stick allow it to point toward the person holding the stick? Not if one assumes the cue stick was held nearly horizontally, but if it was held vertically, the gun could have spun about and fired in any direction. One volunteer experimenter's test results showed that the gun would, in fact, point toward the cue-stick holder more often than not, due to the weight of the hand grip.

A technical discussion of the merits of the story:
www.DarwinAwards.com/book/cue.html

DISQUALIFIED DARWIN AWARD:
MIDNIGHT SNACK

Confirmed by Darwin
23 OCTOBER 2002, AUSTRALIA

What, besides beer, is Australia's most recognizable symbol? Salt-water crocodiles, of course, as popularized by "Crocodile Hunter" Steve Irwin. And what is the most popular tourist activity? Why, viewing these amazing beauties in their natural habitat!

Tourists from around the world visit the wild places of Australia in search of reptilian predators, so open water is routinely posted with graphic warning signs that remind people that swimming with these carnivores is not a good idea. The signs typically show a human figure caught between the jaws of a "saltie." The blunt graphic has proven quite effective . . . at least, until now.

As usual, the billabong was clearly posted with toothy danger signs. As usual, Gondwana Adventure Tours had presented an hour of safety instruction. Despite these precautions a young German woman was about to get more adventure than she bargained for that warm spring evening.

Police Commander Max Pope stated, "The warm night, the full moon . . . the billabong looked idyllic." But danger in the form of a twelve-foot saltie lurked beneath the tranquility. The next morning "the crocodile was located still holding the deceased. It was harpooned by wildlife officers."

For both woman and crocodile the idyllic days of summer ended with a midnight snack.

Reference: Reuters

Darwinian Rule Violation:
No astounding misapplication of judgment.

News reports revealed that the tour guide had assured his group that it was safe to swim in the billabong, as only a less aggressive species of freshwater crocodiles was found in it. The guide himself had swum there earlier that day. A Northern Territory court found the tour guide guilty of "committing a dangerous omission" causing the woman's death. Therefore, the tourist was victim of bad information from a trusted source and is not eligible for a Darwin Award.

Crocodiles once fled from humans, but frequent contact and a ban on hunting has caused them to lose their fear, and tourist boats are compounding the danger by teaching them to jump for food. What kind of wine goes with German food?

DISQUALIFIED DARWIN AWARD:
ROCK CLIMBING PRIORITIES

Confirmed by Darwin

26 JULY 2002, ALASKA

Cell phones are a mixed blessing. Most drivers have seen the person ahead veer dangerously while attempting to steer and talk at the same time. Distraction can be deadly, but cell phones also save lives, especially in southeast Alaska, where there are few roads and most of the land is wilderness. Help can be far away, especially without the ability to make emergency calls. So cell phones are both blessing and curse, and recently a cell phone was an accessory in the death of a rock climber.

Rock climbing is an inherently dangerous sport, and some of the most dangerous ascents lie in the mountains of the Coast Range dividing the Alaskan Panhandle from Canada. Just the act of *surveying* that rugged international border was a heroic calling at the turn of the century. Brave men ventured off the known map, climbed the mountains with glass plate cameras, and invented "aerial photography" while still earthbound.

One border point the surveyors never climbed was Devil's Thumb, northeast of the Norwegian fishing community of Petersburg. The mountain is aptly named, as it resembles a vertical thumb trying to hitch a ride in the sky. It is over nine thousand feet high, and there is no easy ascent. It was first climbed in 1946, and while there have been thirty-seven attempts since, only fourteen expeditions have reached the summit.

Part of the difficulty lies with the climate. The Alaskan Panhandle is a temperate rain forest with up to 162 inches of rainfall a year. In the mountains that translates to dozens of feet of snow, and the inclement weather that goes along with incessant snowfall.

The three tenets of rock climbing are teamwork, safety, and belaying. These are especially important on a mountain as difficult as Devil's Thumb, where weather, isolation, and terrain mean help can be days away, even with the instant communication offered by a cell phone.

Yet a thirty-year-old climber left his team behind and climbed solo because he wanted "to improve reception on his cell phone." Fifty feet up from the base camp at seven thousand feet, he had his cell phone in his hand when he disturbed a rock, started a landslide, and was buried under tons of gravel and boulders.

When his companions were told that it was impossible to retrieve his body, they agreed that the mountain was a fitting burial place for the avid climber who died doing what he loved. It was not clear whether they were referring to mountain climbing or to speaking on the cell phone.

Reference: *Juneau Empire*, *Ketchikan Daily News*, Alaska Public Radio

Darwinian Rule Violation:
No astounding misapplication of judgment.

Due to poor weather two of the deceased's climbing companions had already been helicoptered off the mountain, but the helicopters were not able to return for another pickup due to worsening conditions. This climber was not trying to get better reception for a frivolous call, but rather for a very serious emergency call to determine when he could expect to be rescued. Extreme-sports enthusiasts know they are taking risks, but we do not give Darwin Awards to people simply for engaging in risky sports. Therefore this story does not qualify for a Darwin Award.

**Read a moving account of the climb
by a fellow mountaineer.
www.DarwinAwards.com/book/rockclimbing.html**

DISQUALIFIED DARWIN AWARD:
SLICK SHIT SLIP

Confirmed by Darwin
17 APRIL 2002, ARIZONA

Had he been eating too many banana peels? A Mohave County Jail inmate defecated on his cell floor, slipped in his own feces, struck his head on the ground, and died. The forty-nine-year-old had been arrested for trespassing the previous week. Astoundingly, a sheriff's spokesperson said that "foul play had been ruled out." Felled by your own feces? I'd call that foul!

Reference: www.azcentral.com, Associated Press

Darwinian Rule Violation:
No astounding misapplication of judgment.

To defecate in one's jail cell is certainly in poor taste, but it's hardly an error that the average person expects to end in death. To slip and fall in one's own excrement is certainly an error but hardly an astoundingly stupid one. And so, while this story is amusing, mostly because of its setting and the bathroom humor quotient, it's not fit fodder for a Darwin Award.

Disqualified Darwin Award:
Speed Bump

Confirmed by Darwin
8 August 2001, Texas

At midnight an Arlington publican was forced to refuse further alcoholic drinks to an intoxicated bar patron who was known as a violent drunk. But the bartender halted the flow too late. The irate troublemaker threw a woman to the floor before he was subdued by other patrons, who ejected him from the bar.

The sheriff was summoned to head off further problems.

When squad cars approached the scene, on the lookout for a pugnacious drunk, they encountered an extra speed bump—which turned out to be the miscreant, passed out in the center turn lane of the highway adjacent to the bar.

The deceased receives the "Best Imitation of a Speed Bump" Award.

Reference: *Arlington Star-Telegram*

Darwinian Rule Violation:
No astounding misapplication of judgment.

This story was submitted with an amusing write-up, but it's essentially the story of a man who was so falling-down drunk that he, well, he fell down. That's not smart, but it's not an incredibly stupid decision either. Furthermore, it's common for people to drink enough to pass out. The only astonishing feature of the story is that the "Speed Bump" was a mean drunk who happened to slump in the middle of a highway. Therefore, no Darwin Award.

Disqualified Honorable Mention: Life's a Gas

Confirmed by Darwin

28 January 2001, Japan

A man attempting to commit suicide brought a tank of propane into his apartment, opened its stopcock, and waited to die. Instead, he merely lost consciousness. Four hours later he revived and, forgetting the suicide attempt, lit a cigarette. The explosion blew out an apartment wall and burned the face of the suicidal smoker.

Reference: *Mainichi Daily News*

Darwinian Rule Violation:
Suicide attempt.

The man may have thought the tank contained carbon monoxide instead of propane, despite the label. Even if the tank had been filled with carbon monoxide, however, the suicide attempt was destined to fail unless he had shut himself inside a small, tightly sealed space. Apartments are ventilated, and the gas would dissipate fairly rapidly. Outside air exchange during his period of unconsciousness explains why the propane explosion was not more severe. Regardless of what gas he thought he was inhaling, suicide attempts are not Darwin worthy.

DISQUALIFIED HONORABLE MENTION:
TAINTED TURKEY
Confirmed by Darwin
23 NOVEMBER 2000, CONNECTICUT

A family tradition spiraled into disaster when a meat thermometer exploded in a roasting turkey on Thanksgiving Day. The family of five decided to eat the turkey anyway, and in short order they were dialing for an ambulance. The family was rushed to the hospital, treated, and released. Officials are still trying to determine what chemical was in the thermometer. Looks like we can expect a new warning label next year: "Contents of this thermometer are not to be used as a condiment."

Darwinian Rule Violation:
Innocent bystanders injured.
No astounding misapplication of judgment.

It's unlikely that the entire family was involved in the decision to eat the turkey, so innocent bystanders were injured. In any case, the decision to eat the turkey was not really all that stupid, as a cook might well assume that a meat thermometer is safe to use with food, even if it breaks. Furthermore, the family may simply have been poor, hungry people taking a chance with the only food available to them. For these reasons they do not deserve an Honorable Mention.

Most meat thermometers contain no liquid. Pop-up meat thermometers are spring loaded with a dab of glue that holds the spring and dissolves at the proper temperature. Others use a bimetallic zinc/copper strip, like a heater thermostat. The type of kitchen thermometer that does contain ominous red liquid is simply filled with alcohol with a red colorant, which is far safer than mercury.

DISQUALIFIED HONORABLE MENTION:
WILD MUSHROOMS

A near–Darwin experience happened at Thanksgiving in the small town of Shamrock. A couple were invited to Thanksgiving dinner with friends, and they decided to bring a treat. So they went wild-mushroom picking and cooked a casserole to share with their hosts.

Keep reading—it's not what you think!

The rest of the table was hesitant to try the cheesy concoction, and they uneasily joked about poisonous mushrooms. But the chef assured them that he was an experienced mycologist and knew the difference between good and bad mushrooms. Convinced, the others eventually dug in.

After the main meal was cleared, the leftover casserole was scraped into the cat's dish, and the family feline promptly cleaned his plate. About the time that the dessert dishes were being taken to the kitchen, someone noticed the family cat making odd noises and mewling slightly. Sick cat!

His illness pushed everyone into a poisonous-mushroom panic. The Thanksgiving party piled into vehicles and rushed to the hospital, where several stomachs were pumped.

When they returned home, weak but thankful to be alive, they found that the cat had not been in the throes of a deadly poison at all—in fact, quite the opposite. She had given birth to three kittens in their absence.

Darwinian Rule Violation:
No astounding misapplication of judgment.
Lacks veracity.

This story is probably an Urban Legend, as numerous variants have been reported. It has been seen reenacted by Tom Selleck and by John Cleese, and heard from an eighth-grade teacher. It took place with a salmon instead of mushrooms, or the cat was injured by a neighbor's car. Whether true or false, the precipitous but unnecessary flight to the emergency room is amusing. But the participants didn't make phenomenally bad decisions— on the contrary, their pell-mell rush to the hospital was a cogent decision that could have saved their lives—so no Honorable Mention for this story.

Mushroom species produce peculiar toxins.

Coprinus atramentarius, commonly called "inky cap," and *Clitocybe clavipes* inhibit the alcohol metabolism pathway. The result: Tiny amounts of alcohol (such as a chocolate cordial) cause inebriation and a glass of wine can kill. Nevertheless, these mushrooms are considered a delicacy by gourmands. The effects of these toxins are similar to Antabuse, a drug used to help alcoholics control their drinking.

Amanita phalloides mushrooms inhibit DNA production. Liver and kidney cells, which divide rapidly, are particularly vulnerable. Symptoms of poisoning begin four to twelve hours after ingestion and include nausea, stomach pain, and diarrhea. The unlucky sufferer appears to recover for a few days, but it is a false recovery. Liver and kidney functions continue to decline, and hepatic and renal failure cause death approximately a week after ingestion.

Some species of mushrooms are deliberately ingested for the psychoactive effects of their toxins. In religious ceremonies, *Amanita muscaria,* is consumed widely by Asians, and *Psylocybe* species by indigenous Americans. A distinguishing feature of the psylocybin mushroom is that it turns blue-green where it has been touched.

Appendices

1. Website Biography

The Darwin Awards archive was born on a Stanford University webserver in 1994. Its cynical view of the human species made it a favorite speaker in classrooms, offices, and pubs around the world. News of the website spread by word of mouth, and submissions flew in from far and wide. As the archive grew, so did its acclaim.

The website matriculated to its own domain in 1997, won dozens of Internet awards, and now ranks among the top 3,000 most-visited websites. It currently entertains approximately half a million visitors per month in its comfortable Silicon Valley home. Guests are welcome to set off fireworks and play on the trampoline.

www.DarwinAwards.com is the locus for official Darwin Awards and related tales of misadventure. New accounts of terminal stupidity appear daily in the public Slush Pile. Visitors can vote on stories, sign up for a free email newsletter, and share their opinions on the Philosophy Forum—a community of free thinkers who enjoy numerous philosophical, political, and scientific conversations.

Some stories in this book include a URL directing you to a webpage with more information. All of the hyperlinks can be explored starting from this portal:

www.DarwinAwards.com/book/book3links.html

2. Author Biography

Wendy Northcutt studied molecular biology at UC Berkeley, worked in a neuroscience research laboratory at Stanford, and later joined a biotech startup developing cancer and diabetes therapeutics. She launched the Darwin Awards archive while waiting for her experiments to run their courses.

Eventually Wendy abdicated her laboratory responsibilities in favor of a more off-beat career. She now works as a freelance webmaster and public speaker, and hones her technical skills on the Darwin Awards website. In her free time she studies human behavior, and forms eccentric opinions while traveling, gardening, and glassblowing.

Wendy first learned of the concept of the Darwin Awards from her cousin Ian, a free spirit who later started his own religion in order to avoid shaving his beard while working in the pizza industry. Ian is now pursuing a degree in archeology, and his hair is not an issue.

3. List of Illustrations

Twelve illustrations in this book were created by cartoonist and animation producer Malcolm McGookin. Malcolm, a former *Dangermouse* and *Count Duckula* animator, creates cartoons and illustrations for markets as diverse as children's books and *Penthouse* magazine.

Six illustrations in this book were created by Jay "Zeebarf" Ziebarth, an Internet cartoonist and award-winning *Flash* designer. Jay is currently developing a top-secret television show.

For color versions of the cartoons, more illustrations, and a chance to compliment the artists on their work, visit:

www.DarwinAwards.com/book/mcgookin.html
www.DarwinAwards.com/book/zeebarf

Story Index